FAITH AND POLITICS
MATTERS

NOVALIS

© 2015 Novalis Publishing Inc.

Cover design: Blair Turner
Layout: Audrey Wells

Published by Novalis

Publishing Office
10 Lower Spadina Avenue, Suite 400
Toronto, Ontario, Canada
M5V 2Z2

Head Office
4475 Frontenac Street
Montréal, Québec, Canada
H2H 2S2

www.novalis.ca

Cataloguing in Publication is available from Library and Archives Canada.

Printed in Canada.

All rights reserved. No part of this publication may be reproduced, stored in a retrieval system, or transmitted in any form, or by any means, electronic, mechanical, photocopying, recording, or otherwise, without the written permission of the publisher.

We acknowledge the financial support of the Government of Canada through the Canada Book Fund for business development activities.

5 4 3 2 1   19   18   17   16   15

MIX
Paper from responsible sources
FSC
www.fsc.org   FSC® C103567

Contents

Introduction: Politics Matters • John Milloy 5

Chapter 1: Religion, Politics, and the State in Canada:
A Historical Perspective • Mark McGowan 15

Chapter 2: The Other Solitude: Quebec,
the Charter of Values, and Reasonable
Accommodation • Jean-François Laniel 30

Chapter 3: Classroom Politics:
Public Catholic Education • Kevin Feehan 43

Chapter 4: From the Gates of the New Jerusalem to
the Taste of Ashes: Reflections on Political Activism
and Faith • Peter Warrian 67

Chapter 5: Faith and Politics:
Reflections from the Front Line • John Milloy 76

Chapter 6: Telling Religion to "Shut Up" • Scott Kline 89

Chapter 7: Public Ethics as a Canadian
"Public Theology" • David Pfrimmer 104

Endnotes 129

Introduction

POLITICS MATTERS

John Milloy

John Milloy is a former Ontario Provincial Cabinet Minister who served as Member of Provincial Parliament for Kitchener Centre from 2003 to 2014. Prior to that, he worked on Parliament Hill in Ottawa, including five years in the Office of Prime Minister Jean Chrétien, where he served as Legislative Assistant. He is currently the co-director of the Centre for Public Ethics and assistant professor of public ethics at Waterloo Lutheran Seminary, and the inaugural practitioner in residence in Wilfrid Laurier University's political science department. He is also a lecturer in the Master of Public Service program at the University of Waterloo.

He holds a doctorate in modern history from Oxford University and an M.A. in international history from the London School of Economics.

It seems almost everyone's parents told them that religion and politics were topics (along with sex) that never made for polite conversation. As both were intensely private and personal, and beliefs varied, we were advised to talk about the weather instead. The proposition that these two forbidden subjects might somehow be related was certainly beyond many people's comprehension.

Although some of the taboos around discussing these topics individually may be disappearing, we still seem to hold to the belief that politics and religion don't mix. The argument is well rehearsed. We live in a diverse society with a wide range of faith traditions, including many who profess no religious beliefs. Politicians cannot be seen as favouring a particular religious faith or trying to impose the views of one tradition on society. "Separation of church and state," although originally an American concept, continues to have great resonance in Canada.

The goal of this volume is to challenge this notion by firmly taking the position that faith and politics do go together and, as the title suggests, they matter.

In entering into this debate, the authors of this volume are joining a discussion that has taken place for several thousand years, with no final resolution. From Augustine's Two Cities to Luther's Two Kingdoms to Richard John Neuhaus's Naked Public Square, thinkers have struggled with the question of the relationship between religious beliefs and how we organize ourselves politically.

Although there are instances in the Old Testament of God directly assisting political rulers, there are also many examples of prophets calling on society and its leaders to undergo dramatic transformation. The New Testament seems to offer similar contradictions. In some ways, Jesus was a very political figure in a highly charged environment, and yet, to the disappointment of many of his followers, his mission did not involve wholesale political change.

"Render therefore unto Caesar the things which are Caesar's; and unto God the things that are God's" is an admonition open to interpretation. Does this mean that we should focus on our faith and leave politics to the politicians? Or, based on wider Christian teaching, should we recognize the power of politics to transform our world in ways that are consistent with Christ's teachings?

The words of Charles Davis suggest the latter course. The eminent religious thinker pointed out that "[t]he Christian religion has always been thoroughly political … Christians find God in their neighbour rather than in their consciousness or in the cosmos."[1] If Davis is right, then we need to learn how to live with that neighbour in a peaceful, life-giving way. This in turn requires the establishment of a political system in which persons of faith can contribute. As Pope Francis recently stated, "A good Catholic meddles in politics, offering the best of himself, so that those who govern can govern."[2]

There are many challenges. As Canada becomes increasingly diverse, with a growing population that either claims no religious affiliation or self-identifies as atheist or agnostic, the notion of religion as a purely private affair is gaining ground. The state, many argue, should remain neutral and give no voice to religion.

There is nothing wrong with the concept of a neutral state or respecting the beliefs of all citizens. What began, however, as an exercise in levelling the playing field is in danger of becoming a system that favours those views and opinions that come from a non-religious perspective over those inspired by faith. John Lennon's advice, contained in his song "Imagine," that a world without "religion" or "heaven" or "hell" would result in all of us living a "life in peace" is increasingly becoming accepted wisdom in many corners.

This is unfair to faith communities. The term "secular" should refer to a society that is inclusive of all views but favours none, not a society that excludes the faithful.

It is also unfair to society itself. As we struggle with a mounting list of issues, challenges, and problems, we need all voices present within the public square. With so many of the solutions requiring the acceptance of common responsibility and collective action, the input of those whose central belief is love of neighbour demonstrated through self-sacrifice should be a welcome addition.

This is not simply about organized religion. The growth of those who consider themselves "spiritual but not religious" has created an important segment of the population who believe in a transcendent external truth. They, too, want their voice to be heard in public debates.

Finding a role for faith within our political system has its challenges. Politics, by its very nature, is about compromise. Religious beliefs, on the other hand, tend to be based on accepted truths that are considered timeless and inviolable. How do faith communities and their members navigate the inevitable compromises that are at the essence of most political solutions?

Persons of faith and faith communities also need to be careful. God does not appear to be in the business of endorsing political parties or platforms. Yet, over the course of history, there have been those politicians who have tried to court religious voters by identifying their program with a particular set of religious beliefs. How do faith communities and persons of faith avoid being co-opted into the political system?

And what of the politicians themselves? How does a person of faith who enters elected office effectively represent the diverse group of individuals who elected them, and engage in the inevitable give and take that is part of political life, while staying true to their religious faith?

This is a particularly perplexing question for Canadians. While we often see politicians in the United States enthusiastically wearing their faith on their sleeve, Canada has a different tradition. Despite having elected many individuals with profound religious beliefs, Canadian politicians tend to downplay those beliefs and rarely mention them publicly.

The pages that follow trace the history of these questions in Canada, the experience of those in political life, as well as some tentative suggestions for creating a system that is more welcoming to persons of faith.

Historian Mark McGowan sets the historical stage in the first chapter, outlining the Canadian experience of "Religion, Politics, and the State." Tracing the story back to the 17th-century French settlements, he outlines the close relationship that existed between the state and Canada's principal religious groups until the late 20th century.

Despite the failure of attempts to establish the Church of England as Canada's state church, the influence of many mainline faiths remained strong. Religious influence helped shape much of our nation's policies in four key areas: marriage, education, communications, and social welfare.

McGowan believes that the period following the 1960s was one of "disentanglement" of religion from politics. The influence of religious voters in helping to decide elections began to decline, and he concludes that Canada has been slowly transformed into a country where organized religion plays a minimal role in the public square.

No discussion of religion and politics in Canada can ignore the role that the Catholic Church played within Quebec as well as the speed in which this influence disappeared, to be replaced by the "Reasonable Accommodation Crisis" and "Charter of Quebec Values" controversy of recent years.

In his chapter, "The Other Solitude: Quebec, the Charter of Values, and Reasonable Accommodation," sociologist Jean-François Laniel attempts to make sense of this striking transformation. Laniel provides an overview of the dominance of the Catholic Church in Quebec until the 1960s. As he concludes, "To be Québécois, or more precisely French Canadian, was to be Catholic."

Laniel believes that it was in fact because of this domination that the reaction against religious faith during the Quiet Revolution of the 1960s was so dramatic. He contrasts the Quebec experience with those countries where there was no dominant religion but instead had several Protestant faiths. He believes that due to the already diverse nature of these societies, it was much easier to ease into a growing separation of church and state and adopt notions of individual worship and religious freedom than in a closed Catholic society like Quebec.

Education can often be a key area of church-state cooperation. In his work, "Classroom Politics: Public Catholic Education," lawyer Kevin Feehan provides a systematic overview of the history of publicly funded Catholic education in Canada, noting that some form of Catholic schooling has existed in Canada since the earliest European settlers.

The question of denominational schools, particularly Catholic ones, was a key issue in the Confederation debates, resulting in a specific section of the *British North America Act* outlining protections in this area. Many argue that Confederation itself was only possible due to this agreement over religious education.

Feehan traces the history of Catholic education in each province and territory, and examines the loss of publicly funded Catholic education in Quebec and in Newfoundland and Labrador. He concludes that Catholic education is an important part of Canadian history and has made an ongoing contribution to the variety, divergence, and strength of our education system.

What of persons of faith who are directly involved in the political process? How have they managed to deal with an increasingly diverse and at times anti-religious society as they carry out their role in public life? The volume contains two essays that attempt to answer that question.

In a very personal essay, economist Peter Warrian writes of the influence of Catholic social teaching on his life and reflects on two meaningful periods where he believed that the "gates of the New Jerusalem" were in sight. He paints a picture of his time as a student activist in the 1960s, describing a movement where at first, "religion was accepted as a common intellectual and spiritual background for all the activists I knew and worked with." Later, he points out, political ideology began to dominate, and religion was relegated to the sidelines.

The election of a New Democratic Party government in Ontario 1990 was the other period where Warrian saw the potential for society to be transformed into one that provided greater economic justice, particularly for workers. The results proved otherwise. Warrian, who served as chief economist to the new government, outlines the tensions between government, labour, and social movement activists that prevented progress, as well as the inability to identify shared values. In the years following, he realized that "we do not build the kingdom; God does," and concludes that a different sort of spirituality may hold the truth to functioning with others in our complex world.

I also enter into the discussion with a personal reflection on my time as both an elected politician and a political adviser. Refusing to check my faith at the door, I speak about some of the challenges I faced as a person of faith in the world of politics. It is a place where religion is often viewed suspiciously or caricatured. This is unfortunate, I point out, outlining a number of important challenges facing Canada where a faith perspective could make a meaningful contribution. Faith also has a positive role to play in providing an anchor for elected officials, who are buffeted by so many forces in the modern world.

As a political advisor and politician, I also struggled with a Catholic Church that often seemed inordinately focused on issues of abortion and gay, lesbian, bisexual, transgender, queer (LGBTQ) rights, to the detriment of what seemed like more pressing matters: poverty and workers' rights; the fair treatment of immigrants and refugees; international peace and security; the rights of Indigenous peoples; human trafficking; and the protection of the environment. As much as any of the traditional hot-button topics, these are also important issues that should influence how persons of faith vote.

The political world is complex and involves compromise. Both voters and faith communities must recognize that translating one's faith into action does not always lead to clear and simple answers. People of faith must be welcomed to the table, but they need to understand the realities of governing a diverse society such as Canada.

Where to go from here? In a provocatively titled essay, "Telling Religion to Shut Up," religious studies professor and author Scott Kline bemoans the fact that too much of the debate around religion and politics has been "filtered through the distorted rhetoric of the 'culture wars.'" It seems to be less about trying to find a balance between religion and politics and more about using religion as a political weapon to attack the other side, particularly in debates over issues related to reproduction and sexuality.

Kline argues that the rhetoric of these culture wars has led to oversimplification. Too many people, he believes, try to divide the world into "traditionalists," who want to impose Christian values on society, and "secularists," who want to exclude religion from the public square. Kline believes that the situation is much more nuanced and that there is room for dialogue and cooperation. As society becomes more diverse and less religious, persons of faith need to be able to "translate their moral and political values into a common language – the language of public reason…." At the same time, society itself must more readily accept the religious perspective.

Public ethicist David Pfrimmer provides the final chapter of the book – a thoughtful piece on the potential that public ethics has in encouraging a greater role for people of faith within Canadian society. His essay begins by highlighting recent controversies that have captivated public attention: from the Senate expense scandal to charges against CBC radio personality Jian Ghomeshi to the shooting in Ferguson, Missouri.

Pfrimmer believes that these instances create "ethical moments" where we can collectively engage in moral engagement and deliberation as voluntary associations of individuals or "publics." Such an exercise in public ethics can have a theological dimension as people seek to "find meaning in our current context" by drawing upon their deepest values and convictions, whether these are religiously based or not.

For Pfrimmer, this coming together to address the ethical dimensions of our society's major issues could help bridge the divide between the traditionally faithful and those who consider themselves "spiritual but not religious." It has the potential to create a true public theology that in turn could help us reimagine a more relevant role in the public square for Canada's churches and people of faith.

Canada is a country that faces great challenges. It is also a diverse nation representing a long list of faith traditions, perspectives, and attitudes, ranging from devout followers of established religions to those who feel "spiritual but not religious" to those who are antagonistic to religious faith. We need not only to find a way for all these attitudes to co-exist peacefully, but also to find a path that will allow all of them to contribute to our greater well-being. This volume provides some insights and food for thought as we struggle as a nation to understand the important and complex relationship between faith and politics.

Chapter 1

RELIGION, POLITICS, AND THE STATE IN CANADA: A HISTORICAL PERSPECTIVE

Mark McGowan

Mark McGowan is a principal emeritus of the University of St. Michael's College and a professor of history at the University of Toronto. He has written several award-winning books and articles on the history of the Catholic Church in Canada, immigration, and ethnicity, and has just completed a new book on Canada's Irish Catholics and the Great War. His most recent book for Novalis was *Death or Canada: The Irish Famine Migration to Toronto, 1847*.

In 2001, the Canadian and United States governments chose different ways to officially mourn the loss of life in New York City when terrorists destroyed the two towers of the World Trade Center and most of its occupants on September 11. In Washington, DC, president George W. Bush presided at a ceremony of national mourning in the Episcopalian Cathedral. At the service, Christian clergy, a rabbi, and an imam offered prayers and reflections. There was an air of sanctity, national unity, and the underlying emphasis on religious toleration to which America aspired. At the same time, in Canada, national leaders gathered on the front lawn of Parliament Hill in Ottawa. After reflections by the Governor General and other lay persons, instead of prayer there was a moment of silence in which each participant on the Hill and those watching the ceremony on television could offer whatever prayer or thoughts they deemed appropriate. A visitor from another world, upon viewing both ceremonies, would have been hard pressed to identify which of the two emanated from the Enlightenment republic, whose constitution reinforces the complete separation of church and state. Ironically, it was the Canadian ceremony that appeared to be the product of such thought, despite the fact that there was never any formal separation of church and state in Canada, and that historically, politics and religion had been comfortable bedfellows.

Until the late 20th century, Canadian politics and the state had a close relationship with the country's principal religious groups. In the colonial period, the Catholic Church and the Protestant churches followed the European principle of *cuius regio, eius religio* (the religion of the prince is the religion of the place). In 1627, the French monarchy forbade the emigration of Protestant Huguenots to New France. Roman

Catholicism was formally established in French America when François de Laval was elected the first Vicar Apostolic (1658), later Bishop (1674), of Quebec.[1] This religious establishment lasted until the British military conquest of New France in 1763, which provided the foundation for the Church of England to be established across the conquered territories in what was now British North America. Anglican bishops were appointed for Halifax and Quebec, which were precursors to future Anglican dioceses in St. John's, Montreal, Kingston, and Toronto. While the intent of the Anglican establishment was to replicate church–state relations as they existed in England and Scotland, the formal rules and features of Anglican ascendancy never took root in British North America. In 1791, the new *Constitution Act*, which created Upper and Lower Canada (Ontario and Quebec), gave the Church of England exclusive control over marriage, state funding for clergy and rectories, and one seventh of all Crown land as clergy reserve; by the 1850s, the establishment was in tatters.[2] French-Canadian Catholics refused to relinquish their faith, while dissident Protestant immigrants from the United States and Britain – Methodists, Baptists, Congregationalists, and many Presbyterians – swamped the small Anglican population, rendering its aspirations of social control in British North America irrelevant.

One reason for the failure of the Protestant establishment could be the manner in which the British Crown recognized the collective rights of Canada's Roman Catholics. Prior to the Conquest of Canada in 1763, Catholics within the British Empire were subject to the Test Acts and Penal Laws, which effectively stripped them of property rights, the liberty to aspire to the liberal professions, the right to vote, and the right to sit in elected assemblies. The Penal Laws applied in most British Colonies, except in what would become Ontario and Quebec. Under the Articles of Capitulation of 1760, and confirmed by the Treaty of Paris in 1763, the Roman Catholic faith was permitted in the Old Province of Quebec "so far as the laws of Great Britain permit."[3] As a result of a liberal reading of the Act by the first British governors of Quebec, a new Catholic bishop of Quebec was appointed in 1766, in consultation with Rome and with the approval of the British Government. Catholicism, now tolerated, remained as an unofficial establishment in Quebec. As the thirteen American colonies pushed themselves to the brink of open revolt, the British government hoped to keep the northern colonies loyal. The passage of the *Quebec Act* in 1774 acknowledged the collective rights of Catholics and retained seigneurial tenure, French civil law, the Church's right to tithe, and the formal extension of civil rights to Catholics in the conquered territory.[4] In 1791, these rights passed to the new province of Upper Canada (Ontario), which was carved out of the province of Quebec; thereafter, Catholics voted and sat in provincial assemblies, becoming some of the very few in the British Empire accorded these rights.

Ironically, Catholics in the rest of the British Empire would not witness the same freedoms accorded to Canadians until Catholic Emancipation in 1829. Until that time, Catholics in the Atlantic colonies of Newfoundland, Prince Edward Island, New Brunswick, and Nova Scotia did not have the same civil and political rights as their co-religionists in Upper and Lower Canada. This exclusion from the political process tended to make Catholics feel jaded towards the provincial governments in several colonies that tended to be run by Conservative or Tory alliances, sympathetic to the privileges of the Crown. In Nova Scotia, emancipation was advanced when Cape Breton was merged with the mainland in 1820 and Lawrence Kavanagh, a Roman Catholic from the newly added territory, attempted to take his seat in the colonial legislature. The Assembly decided to exempt Kavanagh from the sections of the oath of office, which was offensive to Catholics because of its denial of transubstantiation. After a campaign to have the test oaths suppressed for Nova Scotia, Catholic emancipation was effected in the province two years before the rest of the British Empire.[5]

What the colonial period provides for Canada is foundations recognizing that religious minorities possessed collective rights and that models of church establishment were inappropriate. By the 1850s, what emerged was a principle of voluntaryism in which no religious group would be formally established by the state, and citizens were at liberty to profess whatever faith they wished. Canada would witness a broad Christian consensus, engaging five major religious denominations – Roman Catholic, Anglican, Methodist, Presbyterian, and Baptist – which assumed that Canada would be a Christian country in its values, public morality, and laws.[6] While these denominations, which historically constituted over 80 percent of Canadians, witnessed moments of tension – even violence – between one another, there seemed to be little doubt that they were guardians of the public good and were co-responsible with the nation's politicians to maintain the peace, order, and good government of Canada. In general, religious influence intersected with Canadian politics in four areas: marriage, education, communications, and social welfare.

On the subject of marriage, the major Canadian Christian denominations acknowledged that the family was the bedrock of society. There was no question, after the failure of the Anglican monopoly over presiding at marriages, that all Christian denominations, serving as both religious presiders and civil officials, would be accorded the right to officially marry couples. Divorce, once anathema in all major churches, was severely regulated and permitted only by a bill in Parliament. As a result, Canada had one of the lowest rates of divorce in the Western world. Homosexuality and abortion were included in the Criminal Code until 1968. The churches also weighed in heavily on social issues that would inevitably prey upon the family and threaten society. The production and distribution of alcohol was a hotly contested issue that was spearheaded by Protestant Christians, particularly through such agencies as the Women's Christian Temperance Union (WCTU), which pressured politicians to prohibit the production and sale of beer, wine, and liquor in Canada. The WCTU, some Protestant clergy, and temperance-oriented politicians managed to effect prohibition, except in Quebec, during later phases of the Great War (1914–1918) and into the early 1920s.[7] While prohibition was ultimately repealed, except in counties exercising the local option under the *Scott Act* (1878), provincial control of alcohol and beer sales remained tightly controlled, much to the approval of the more conservative Protestant Christians. In a similar move to regulate public morality, in 1906, a Protestant Christian movement called The Lord's Day Alliance managed to influence the passage of the *Lord's Day Act*, which effectively prohibited work on Sundays in Canada. Christian churches, in cooperation with politicians of all political stripes, had preserved Sunday as a day of rest for Canadian families.[8]

Perhaps the most profound influence of the Christian churches on the Canadian state and its politicians was the collective rights accorded to religious groups in the area of public education. Few Canadians in the pre-Confederation period would have contemplated a system of public education in Canadian provinces that did not have religion constituting its moral base. In Ontario, the fathers of public education, Anglican Bishop John Strachan of Toronto and Methodist minister Egerton Ryerson, Superintendent of Education from 1844 to 1871, were adamant that prayer and Christian instruction be woven into the fabric of Ontario's public school curriculum.[9] Tensions between Protestants and Catholics in most colonies, and each group's fear of the other controlling the education of their children, prompted the creation of separate publicly funded denominational schools. This initiative, established in the United Province of Canada under the *Day Act* of 1841, permitted the creation of separate schools for the Protestant minority in what is now Quebec and for the Roman Catholic minority in what is now Ontario. This compromise reflected an attention to collective rights, acknowledged in the *Quebec Act* (1774), and to keeping the peace between religious groups in Canada. By the time of Canadian Confederation, separate schools for both Protestants and Catholics enjoyed public funding, enshrined under Section 93 of the *British North America Act* (now the *Constitution Act*). Section 93 ensured that if the provinces, which are responsible for education, trod upon the rights of religious minorities, the federal government could intervene to protect minority rights.[10] Because these rights in the Maritime provinces were not established "in law" but by gentleman's agreement, publicly funded separate schools were not protected by the *British North America Act*; provinces eventually abandoned their support of these schools. Charles Tupper, a Protestant Conservative politician from Nova Scotia, considered Section 93 a vital component in the success of the Confederation agreement.[11] Similar educational rights were extended to Manitoba (1870) and the Northwest Territories, large sections of which eventually became Saskatchewan and Alberta.

Christian churches were also effective in making certain that public morality and religious balance were maintained in social communications. Churches owned their own newspapers and used their influence with political parties to ensure a modicum of decency in newspapers run by the Liberal and Conservative parties. With the rise of cinema, modern theatre, and burlesque theatre in the early 20th century, local clergy kept politicians accountable for acceptable standards of public decency. In Quebec, for example, some Catholic bishops protested the performances of French actress Sarah Bernhardt and later prohibited the screening of the motion picture *Martin Luther* in the province.[12] With the advent of radio, Canadian churches and some rabbis were eager to use the new medium as an electronic pulpit. Once again, churches engaged with politicians to effect national policies of decency and balance on the airwaves. In 1928, the International Bible Students Association (IBSA: Jehovah's Witnesses) ran afoul of the mainline Christian churches with their less-than-tolerant broadcasts over their five radio stations, covering listening audiences in central and western Canada. The federal minister of Marine and Fisheries, P.J. Arthur Cardin, who was then responsible for radio, and his deputy minister (later Senator) Alexander Johnston, abruptly cancelled the IBSA licenses. Although the government placated major Christian churches, opponents of this censorship (notably, the Jehovah's Witnesses and the Loyal Orange Order) viewed the Liberal government's actions as being in collusion with the Catholic

Church, since both Cardin and Johnston were Catholics.[13] Social democrat MP and future leader of the Co-operative Commonwealth Federation (CCF) J.S. Woodsworth was more alarmed by the government's favouring of one religious group over another: "when did we appoint a minister of this government as censor of religious opinions? ... If Bible Students are to be put out of business because they condemn alike Protestants and Catholics, I do not see why the *Sentinel* and the *Catholic Register* should not be suppressed."[14]

In 1928, the clash between politicians over the role of the state and the place of religion on the Canadian airwaves resulted in the creation of a royal commission (the Aird Commission) to investigate all aspects of Canadian broadcasting. While the most significant result of the commission was the recommendation to create public broadcasting in Canada, it strongly advised regulations to prohibit statements of a controversial nature and to prohibit religious speakers from "making an attack upon the leaders or doctrine of another religion."[15] In 1936, the Canadian Broadcasting Corporation (CBC), the principal regulator of the Canadian airwaves, developed regulation 7c, which stipulated that no broadcast might include "abusive comment on race, religion, or creed."[16] In 1938, after repeated violations of section 7c in Toronto, Gladstone Murray, director of the CBC, created the National Religious Advisory Council to improve religious programming and create a balance between Canada's religious groups that wished to be on the air. These historical precedents of restraint and balance have formed a political compromise with regard to broadcast communications in Canada ever since. In the 1950s, for example, the CBC blocked broadcasts of Bishop Fulton Sheen's famous *Life is Worth Living* because it was too Catholic, American in content, and a religious program with commercial sponsorship.[17] In the 1980s, the Canadian Radio-Television and Telecommunications Commission (CRTC) allowed the creation of Vision TV and its presence in regular cable television only because of its intent to create a tolerant balance between all the representative religious groups participating, both Christian and non-Christian.[18] Gone were the days when any singular religious group could strong arm Canadian politicians to censor the views of others.

Finally, through their social activism, Canadian religious groups played a significant role in shaping the Canadian social safety net and forming social democratic political parties. The brutal effects of laissez-faire capitalism – including poor wages, lack of welfare benefits, long working hours, alarmingly dangerous working conditions, child labour, unsanitary and slum-like living conditions for urban labourers, and the impoverishment of farmers and workers in primary industries – prompted both Canadian Protestants and Catholics to pressure governments to use the legislatures of the land to uplift workers and narrow the gaps between rich and poor. Members of the Methodist (later The United Church of Canada), Presbyterian, Baptist, and Anglican churches formed the Social Gospel movement to bring about "Christ's kingdom" now.[19] They pressured politicians and governments to legislate working and living conditions, improve wages and working hours, provide workmen's compensation, and allow for equal access to medical care. The early leaders of the Cooperative Commonwealth Federation (by 1961 the principal constituent of the New Democratic Party) were often Protestant ministers who had been imbued with Social Gospel principles; a former Baptist minister, Tommy Douglas, for example, established the first public health insurance program in Canada, when he served as CCF Premier of Saskatchewan. Roman Catholics, influenced by such papal encyclicals as *Rerum Novarum* (On the Condition of the Working Class, 1891) and *Quadragesimo Anno* (On Social Reconstruction, 1931), and by the co-operative work of the Antigonish Movement and the *Caisse populaire* (credit union) movement, joined the Social Gospellers in their fight for the government to engage social problems in Canada.[20] In 1943, the Catholic bishops confirmed that there was no prohibition on Catholics voting for or joining the CCF. By the 1970s, two Catholic priests, Andy Hogan of Cape Breton and Bob Ogle of Saskatchewan, actually sat as NDP MPs in the House of Commons in Ottawa.[21]

As Canadian society became more secular in the 1960s and 1970s, Canadian religious groups began to lose much of their influence on politicians and on the formation of public policy, particularly in the areas of marriage and the family, education, communications, and social democracy. When the omnibus bill of 1968 liberalized abortion laws and lifted prohibitions on various sexual lifestyles, Justice minister (later Prime Minister) Pierre Elliott Trudeau was clear that the state had no place in "the bedrooms of the nation." Many churches disagreed and continued to fight both federal and provincial governments on the access and financing of abortions in Canada.[22] Conservative Protestant churches, Roman Catholic bishops, and new Muslim Canadians also resisted the liberalization of political and social views regarding the civil rights of lesbian, gay, bisexual, and transgendered (LGBT) Canadians. Opposition to the extension of equal rights to LGBT groups surfaced when the Liberal government of Prime Minister Paul Martin made same-sex marriage legal in Canada in 2005. The Catholic bishops found little solace in the fact that both Martin and several of his Liberal and Conservative predecessors as prime minister – Trudeau, John Turner, Joe Clark, Brian Mulroney, and Jean Chrétien – were all practising Catholics, and in Trudeau's case, devout. Each, as prime minister, was particularly careful to make certain they legislated on behalf of all Canadians, not just Catholics, and none was in the pocket of the bishops. In 1982, when the Social Affairs Commission of the Canadian Conference of Catholic Bishops published *Ethical Reflections*, a scathing indictment of Canadian social and economic policy, Pierre Trudeau shrugged and noted that bishops made "poor economists."[23]

Canadians had come increasingly to see religion as a private matter, with the public square being reserved for complete religious equality, with no religious voice greater than any other. In education, provinces with publicly funded, legally established, constitutionally protected religious schools began to question why the collective religious rights of one group were privileged over those of all other groups. In 1997, both Quebec and Newfoundland requested that the federal government refrain from invoking its remedial powers enshrined in section 93 of the *Constitution Act* as they dismantled religious schools and replaced them with either a single public non-denominational system or secular systems based on language.[24] In Ontario in 2007, the Liberals retained power when the Progressive Conservatives included extended funding for religious schools for non-Catholic groups in their campaign platform. For Ontarians, establishing more religious schools was a non-starter, with more and more voices calling for the abolition of Catholic schools and the imposition of a single public system with French and English branches.[25] Within Canadian secular culture, there had been a shift in thinking and in jurisprudence since the new Charter of Rights and Freedoms (1982), which now gave individual rights greater attention and priority over the collective rights recognized historically in Canada.[26]

The disentanglement of religion from the state has been most pronounced in the province of Quebec, following the Quiet Revolution of the 1960s. Social and economic change, combined with a pronounced sense of nationhood, transformed French Canadians from one of the most churchgoing Catholic cultures on the planet to one of the most non-religious. Churches have emptied in Quebec, to be sold or to become museums and local cultural centres. Education, health care, and social services, once financed by church and state and operated by clergy and religious, have been completely secularized.[27] Most recently, the separatist Parti Québécois attempted to impose a secular charter of values that would effectively ban any religious symbols or religious clothing in the public service – including state health-care institutions, schools, and daycares. In 2014, this Quebec form of French *laïcité* was rejected by the electorate, and within a year a Catholic collegiate in Montreal had won a second victory when the courts upheld its right not to teach the state's imposed religion and values course.

Within this climate of secularity and Canadian unease with the "religious" in the public square, there has also been a shift in alliances between political parties and religious communities. Traditionally, with some regional exceptions (including Newfoundland and Nova Scotia), Roman Catholics had generally supported the Liberal party, which had embodied values of inclusivity for immigrants, religious diversity, and progressive social policy. Irish Catholics could be found in good numbers in the Conservative ranks, although historically Catholics felt uncomfortable in the Conservative party because of its unofficial alliance with the anti-Catholic Orange Order, its ties with English and Protestant elites, and the rejection of the party in Catholic Quebec after Prime Minister Sir John A. Macdonald had allowed the execution of "rebel" Louis Riel in 1885. Social democrats in the CCF and, later, the NDP had attracted voters from across the religious spectrum, including Catholic and Protestant workers in Canada's industrial centres and on the prairies.

In the late 20th century, overt religious links to partisan politics began to disappear as traditional parties shed themselves of ancient religious baggage; some parties, such as the federal Progressive Conservatives, disappeared entirely. Despite its proclivity to elect federal leaders who were Roman Catholic, the Liberal Party of Canada demonstrated no defence to any church, and its most recent leader, Justin Trudeau, offended its traditional Catholic base with his policy of endorsing only federal Liberal candidates who would vote pro-choice on prospective legislation addressing abortion in Canada.[28] With perhaps the exception of former leadership candidate Bill Blaikie, a United Church minister, elected members and rank and file of the New Democratic Party would be hard pressed to comprehend the proposition by Tommy Douglas at the founding party convention in 1961 that they were building a "new Jerusalem."[29] Perhaps only the newly reconstituted Conservative Party has made a conscious effort to earn the support of social conservatives, evangelical Christians, and traditional Roman Catholics. Some pundits have even suggested that Prime Minister Stephen Harper's own membership in the Christian Missionary Alliance Church has helped shore up his party's close relationship with

Evangelical Christians who refute climate change, oppose same-sex marriage, and support restrictions on abortion, among other issues.[30] Such suspicions have been confirmed by Conservative vote-getting strategies and by recent polls.[31] In advance of the 2011 federal election, Angus Reid surveyed self-described Christians and came up with surprising results. Fifty percent of self-identified Roman Catholics outside of Quebec intended to vote Conservative, and only 25 percent planned to vote for the Liberals. Protestants came in slightly higher, at 56 percent for the Conservatives. New Democrats could count on 19 percent of Catholics and 18 percent of Protestants. It should be pointed out that almost equal numbers of atheists and agnostics outside Quebec supported the Conservatives and Liberals (32 percent and 31 percent respectively), and only 25 percent backed the NDP.[32]

In 2011, no political party depended on organized groups of religious voters, as parties had done in the past. Canadian political parties had stepped away from such allegiances, just as Canada – in its self-identification as a free, diverse, multi-cultural, religiously plural, democratic state – had consciously sought no religious identification that might offend one of its many constituent groups. The focus on individual rights in Canadian jurisprudence, as evidenced in the wake of the passage of the Charter of Rights and Freedoms, has witnessed the gradual erosion of the collective rights that had historically buoyed religious groups as active players in the Canadian public square. In his essay "What Happened to a Christian Canada?" American historian Mark Noll concludes, "Canada, which for so long looked much more Christian than Western Europe, and considerably more Christian than its southern neighbour, now appears in its religious character to resemble Europe much more closely than it does the United States."[33]

Chapter 2

THE OTHER SOLITUDE: QUEBEC, THE CHARTER OF VALUES, AND REASONABLE ACCOMMODATION

Jean-François Laniel

Jean-François Laniel is a Ph.D. candidate in sociology at the Université du Québec à Montréal (UQAM). He studies the links between religion and politics, as well as Catholicism and nationalism, in societies with a dominant Christian tradition, especially in so-called small nations. He is the cofounder of the journal *La Relève*, a publication for French-Canadian students.

Debating Religion in Quebec, Europe, and the United States

A lot has been said and written about religion in Quebec in recent years. For a number of political commentators inside and outside the state of Quebec, the Reasonable Accommodation crisis[1] (2007–2008) and the Quebec Charter of Values (2013–2014) expressed the latent intolerance of the Québécois – their reluctance to embrace the religious and cultural diversity of our time.[2] Since the Parti Québécois and the late Action démocratique du Québec[3] were at the forefront of demands to regulate and banish "ostentatious" religious symbols in public institutions (bureaucracies, courts, hospitals, schools, police, etc.) in the name of both State neutrality and common values,[4] Quebec's long-standing nationalism seemed once again at play.[5] According to a 2014 poll, 51% of Québécois approved the Quebec Charter of Values and 68% of French-speaking Québécois favoured the ban of "ostentatious religious signs" in public institutions[6] – with the notable exception of the crucifix that hangs in the Assemblée nationale.

Chauvinism and xenophobia are handy explanations for debates questioning the modalities of *vivre-ensemble*. Sometimes, they are clearly implicated. The French political party Front National, the German popular movement Pediga, and, most obviously, the neo-Nazi Greek party, Golden Dawn, display national irredentism, populism, and racism. However, every dispute over religious and cultural accommodation is far from being inherently reprehensible. Such heated debates about *laïcité* and cultural integration are the norm rather than the exception in most contemporary liberal democracies across Europe and America, where concern about the intermingling of faith and politics is growing. Media coverage can certainly amplify but rarely invent these debates, and bigoted nationalism can certainly invest in them but hardly summarize them. In fact, an incalculable number of books and studies have been written and conducted over the last few decades on that issue, and one could plausibly argue that religious diversity and religious accommodation are now the leading and most funded topics in the social sciences.

In other words, debates over the place and role of religion in the public sphere are recurrent and are expected to have a long future. They stem from a similar context of growing religious diversity, most frequently related to Islam, that questions every historical model of separation of State and religion (or "regimes of *laïcité*") and every politic of cultural integration, from Anglo-Saxon multiculturalism to French republican *laïcité*, from "separatist" *laïcité* to "anticlerical" and "authoritative" *laïcité*, from a *laïcité* of "civic faith" to a *laïcité* of "recognition" and "collaboration."[7] But if individual and communitarian demands for religious "toleration," "autonomy," "tolerance," and "participation"[8] are formulated throughout liberal democracies, each society responds to them differently. In Canada outside of Quebec, where politics of multiculturalism and "moderate secularism"[9] are officially implemented, the openness to religious expressions in the public sphere is nevertheless contrasted.[10] The Liberal Ontario government decided in 2005 to forbid Islamic tribunals arbitrating marital issues and, by extension, the equivalent Jewish and Christian tribunals that existed for decades. Recently, the federal Conservative government of Stephen Harper announced its intention to proscribe the wearing of the niqab during Canadian citizenship ceremonies, arguing that the niqab is "rooted in a culture that is anti-women" and that it is "offensive" for someone to keep their face hidden during the citizenship ceremony. More recently, a vast number of municipalities throughout Canada refused to preventively apply the Supreme Court's decision to proscribe the religious prayer in and before Saguenay's (Quebec) town hall meetings.

As such, an interesting question to ask of the recent debates over religion and cultural diversity in Quebec is how they participate in a near-universal discussion about religion in public institutions, and how this discussion is influenced by a particular historic, religious, and political context – similar to how Canada, Great Britain, and the United States, albeit with a number of similarities, do not share the same policies in regard to religion in the public sphere. A society's take on secularity and *laïcité* is largely rooted in the role religion has historically played in that society. In fact,

> in every country in Europe [and America], the style of political life, the content of public debate on social and ethical problems, the definition of the areas of responsibility of the State and the individual, conceptions of citizenship and the family, visions of nature and environment, but also practical rules of civil behaviour, relationships to money or modes of consumption (etc.) have taken shape in historical-religious contexts which continue (up to a point) to direct them today.[11]

Keeping this in mind, we might better understand Quebec's principal lines of discussion and fracture over religion with the help of five summary questions that run through this chapter:

a) What are the dominant conceptions of religion in Quebec (organized or personal, dogmatic or individual, given or chosen)?

b) What are their correspondent definitions of religious freedom (limited to the private sphere or not)?

c) What are their different interpretations of the State's role regarding religion (what is "State neutrality")?

d) What is the significance and impact of Catholicism's long presence in Quebec (cultural and patrimonial remnants or active religious symbols)?

e) How do these takes on religion and *laïcité* influence the different lectures on cultural and religious growing diversity (is Quebec's model of *laïcité* multicultural, intercultural, or republican)?

But first, a historical-religious *mise en contexte*.

The "Priest-Ridden Province," the Quiet Revolution, and Multiple Modernities

From the 1840s until the 1960s, the Québécois considered themselves a Catholic nation. As in similar stateless nations such as Ireland and Poland, the Catholic Church framed the private and public life of Quebec: rates of religious practice were unanimously high, the Catholic bishops had an influential say in political matters, the Church was in charge of essential public institutions, from hospitals to playgrounds to public schools, and the national icon of the Québécois was John the Baptist (St-Jean-Baptiste). To be Québécois, or more precisely French Canadian, was to be Catholic. In a political and sociological sense, the Catholic Church thus became a "Church-nation": it deeply inculturated and romanized popular culture, defined national identity and collective myths, and institutionalized society, and its autonomy became the autonomy of the nation.[12]

Such a dominant and omnipotent presence of the Church did not go uncontested, especially after the Second World War. For many, the Church could not meet the challenges of the modern world: it had neither the expertise nor the material means to supply the growing demand for education, for example, as access to secondary and post-secondary education was democratized and universalized. More fundamentally, its conservative take on many ethical issues, such as the vote for women, abortion, and the traditional gender division of labour, as well as its predilection for rural and agricultural life, was considered both oppressive and archaic. Throughout Europe and America, counterculture was popular among urban youth, and free-spiritedness was the main slogan. The Catholic Church of Quebec, however, still practised and encouraged censorship over literature and cinema.

A number of recent studies have considerably nuanced the Church's opposition to what is called "modern values,"[13] be they individualism, capitalism, scientific rationality, State intervention, pluralism (religious and political), and, more widely, liberalism. In the spirit of the *aggiornamento* of the Second Vatican Council (1962–1965), many Catholics in Quebec hoped for a modernization of the Church's values – a return to the more evangelical practices of Catholicism: more personal and intimate, more this-worldly oriented, less doctrinal, and less institutionally controlled. Inspired by French scholars, "personalism," or "left-wing Catholicism," was popular among the Québécois clergy (high and low) and the most militant and active lay Catholics.[14] In other words, the growing criticism of the Church's role in Quebec life was more a critique of a certain variant of traditional and highly ritualized Catholicism, couched in "ultramontanism,"[15] than of Catholicism *tout court*. What is now known as the Quiet

Revolution (1960), or the secularization of Quebec's society and its building of a welfare state, was as much, if not more, the work of fervent Catholics who aspired to rejuvenate the Church from the inside. Hence the apparent oxymoron "Quiet" Revolution, which the Catholic Church did not oppose, but in many aspects encouraged.[16] In other words, modern Quebec, its national identity, and its model of *laïcité* were founded both against the Catholic Church and in the name of Catholicism.

Nevertheless, from this 1960s' spring of liberalization and secularization, a new collective myth was born in Quebec, replacing what was until then known as the French Canadians' "predestined role of evangelizing the continent."[17] By the mid-1970s, Quebec's Sunday religious practice was already among the lowest in Europe and the United States; the number of Catholic priests plummeted, and the welfare state replaced the Catholic Church in every institutional sector of public life. In the collective consciousness of the Québécois, the Catholic Church was associated with Quebec's "Great Darkness" (la "Grande noirceur"): namely, archaism and oppression. Even today, the mythical duo of the "Great Darkness" and the "Quiet Revolution" stands as the grid through which Québécois narrate their collective history.

Sociologist David Martin offers a useful conceptualization of the multiple and divergent national paths of secularization, for which variations in religious monopoly or pluralism, and the beliefs of the dominant church, play a key role. "The prime historical circumstance [is] the difference between ... mainly Protestant [countries], where Enlightenment and religion overlapped and even fused, and those countries, mainly Catholic, where Enlightenment and religion clashed."[18]

The countries in which Protestantism is dominant and pluralistic, with a multiplicity of Protestant churches or sects, easily acclimate to (or go hand in hand with) separation of church and state, individual worship, and freedom of religion. On the other hand, countries where Catholicism is dominant tend to see freedom of the secular and the individual as a combat against religion, which is viewed as organic and institutional: until Vatican II, the Catholic Church aspired to build a "counter-society" in opposition to a secular world that was viewed as individualistic, materialistic, and tenaciously atheist. The inherent religious plurality and individualism of Protestant nations tended to produce, when entering modernity, politics of permeability between public and private expressions of faith(s) and politics of multiculturalism. Catholic nations, meanwhile, tended to produce either national (Catholic) churches (Portugal's, Spain's, and Italy's "national-catholicism" under Salazar, Franco, and Mussolini dictatorships) or strong separation between public and private faith (most notably French) and a unitary conception of citizenship, on the model of the unitary and universal Catholic Church: *la République, une et indivisible*.[19] The "war of the two Frances" is typical of Latin Catholic nations, with a structural and enduring opposition between Jacobin-style laicism and Catholic integralism: Quebec's mythical duo, the "Great Darkness" and the "Quiet Revolution", participates in this combat against religion in Catholic contexts.

"Freedom *to* believe" is hence a predominant concern in historically Protestant countries, and "freedom *from* religion" is predominant in historically Catholic countries.[20] In fact, the term *laïcité* is not used in Protestant countries, which use "secularity." And if differences between Catholic and Protestant nations tend to diminish with time,[21] they still impact public policies regarding religion and how people view and comprehend religion: "One nation under God" in the United States, and strong republican *laïcité* and civil religion in France; high numbers of religious practitioners in the United States, and some of the lowest numbers in France.

Religion, Catholicism, and *Laïcité* in Modern Quebec

Among other potent examples of French Québécois' views on religion, jurist Sébastien Grammond recently compared the decisions of the Quebec Court of Appeal and those of the Supreme Court of Canada in four cases regarding religious accommodation (the *Bergevin* case, the *Amselem* case, the *témoins de Jéhovah de Saint Jérôme-Lafontaine* case, and the *Multani* case). In each of these cases, Grammond observed "distinct conceptions of religion, rather than ... distinct conceptions of fundamental rights."[22] For the Quebec Court of Appeal, and for most Québécois judges sitting on the Supreme Court, religion is considered a) one among many potential aspects of individual identity preferences, b) a voluntary and private decision to adhere to a set of rules, c) to which the majority of the population does not have to adhere or be exposed to, d) and therefore, State neutrality implies an equal and hence reserved recognition of religious particularism and accommodation in the public sphere. It is also worth pointing out that State neutrality is a concept used only by Québécois judges.[23] On the other hand, "the Supreme Court ... views religion as an accumulation of deeply held personal convictions rather than a matter of voluntary choice or personal preferences. In this conception, society must tolerate the individual's public manifestations of his or her religion."[24] It can be argued that such a Québécois view of religion was predominantly expressed throughout the "Reasonable

Accommodation" crisis and transpired in the Quebec Charter of Values: in the name of State neutrality and equality, in the name of Quebec's values (gender equality before religious faith), "ostentatious" religious expressions, notably viewed as "proselytizing" were to be banned from public institutions and religious accommodations were to be rigorously framed and supervised.

Moulded by its French-Canadian and Catholic monopolistic background, religion in French Quebec is conceived as a set of church and therefore doctrinal rules that can be in discordance with more privileged social values such as freedom of thought and gender equality (and hence carefully monitored, for they are thought to be frequently obtained against religion), and ultimately a personal choice to be lived as such, in private, with its potential burden.

We could say it is the "hate" dimension of its love-hate relationship with Catholicism,[25] directed against its dogmatic and institutionally controlled dimension. However, this is only half of Quebec's secularization story. After all, why did the Quebec Charter of Values include a clause protecting the heritage of Catholicism, partly subtracting it from strict state neutrality? Why did Québécois members of Parliament unanimously vote in 2008 to keep the crucifix that ostentatiously hangs over the president of the Assemblée nationale du Québec? And isn't there a contradiction in the treatment of "local" and "foreign" religions, of the "majority" and the "minorities"?

First, as we said earlier, Quebec's modernization coincided with the *aggiornamento* of Vatican II, characterized by its openness to modernity, freedom of conscience, and pluralism; its abdication of proselytism; and its willingness to act as a public service: many have named this process the "internal secularization"[26] of Catholicism, exceptionally present in Quebec.[27] It halted, or rather moderated, the Latin-Catholic pattern of secularization. Second, and this is also noted by Martin, the differentiation process between religion and politics, church and state, is slowed down and different in minorities or small nations. Religion maintains itself as a carrier of identity, as a marker of cultural distinction. These two factors may help us understand the partial and selective incorporation of Catholicism in Quebec's secular culture and institutions after the Quiet Revolution.

This particular role given to Catholicism in modern Quebec can best be seen in the educational system: until 1999, public schools in Quebec were officially Catholic, and the bishops chaired the Catholic committee in charge (2000) of Catholic morality classes, which were taught until 2008. These served as a civic education class. In fact, public schools were placed under a policy called "open confessionalism," which tried to reconcile an inclusive and civic view of nationality and the secularized Catholic preferences of the majority. Catholic dogma was minimal, if not absent, secularized under the umbrella of humanist values; proselytism was proscribed; and toleration to pluralism was an important teaching.[28] In other words, until very recently, Catholicism in Quebec informally played the role of a civil religion, or, more precisely, a "cultural religion."[29]

It is the "love" dimension of Québecois' relationship with Catholicism. Strange as it may seem, for a majority of French Québécois,[30] contemporary Catholicism is not an active religious symbol of faith (indeed, Sunday religious practice is lower in Quebec than in France), but an identity and historical marker: at most, it is a source of universal humanist values that can be shared by every Québécois, independent of private values and faith.[31] As for the strong distinction between the private and public spheres, a similar distinction is made between religious and cultural expressions of religion, and hence between Catholicism and other religious, namely Islam. Religion is hence relegated to the private sphere, and culture elevated to the public sphere. When, in 2007, Cardinal Marc Ouellet, former Archbishop of Quebec, invited Québécois to "remember their baptism" in the face of growing laicist tendencies, his appeal was received with fierce hostility: cultural Catholicism would not be equated with Catholic doctrine and the Catholic Church, which are still remembered as two of the principal figures of the "Great Darkness."[32]

But why all this fuss now? Why did the "Reasonable Accommodation" crisis spark such controversy in 2007–2008, and not before or after? And how does it help us understand, ultimately, "what Quebec wants" in matters of *laïcité*? After all, the debate is not over, for the defeat of the Parti Québécois in the 2014 provincial elections merely postponed any legislation on religious matters.[33]

Naturally, many answers to this question exist: for example, the long-term effects and fear of the September 11, 2001, terrorist attacks, or, for some, one of the many side-effects of Quebec's hard to predict nationalism. But from a historical-religious perspective, the "Reasonable Accommodation" crisis especially coincides with the final removal of the Catholic Church's active role in Quebec's public schools. Up until 2008, Quebec's students in primary and secondary schools had the option of attending either a Catholic religion class (chosen by the majority) or moral instruction; both have been replaced by a common "Cours d'éthique et culture religieuse." And until then, Quebec's debates on religion in the public sphere were framed by the opposition between advocates of *laïcité* and advocates of religious teaching. Since Quebec's public schools removed religion from the curriculum in 2008, partly in the name of a new and more civic public culture (thus creating confusion and discontent when religion comes back under new guises), the debate over religion has moved to how it is known today. Now it presents two variants of *laïcité*, "open" and "strict": the former on the model of Canadian multiculturalism (albeit a provision for French as the official language), known as "interculturalism,"[34] in a way expanding to all religions the historic open tolerance to Catholicism, and the latter on the model of French Republicanism, on the model of the Latin-Catholic pattern (albeit a provision for "cultural Catholicism").

In other words, Quebec's model of *laïcité* has yet to be defined. Now ambivalently balanced between interculturalism and a brand of republicanism, it promises many more debates to come.

Chapter 3

CLASSROOM POLITICS: PUBLIC CATHOLIC EDUCATION

Kevin Feehan

Kevin Feehan is chancellor of Newman Theological College and St. Joseph's Seminary, and the governor and vice-chair of St. Joseph's College at the University of Alberta. A lawyer, he has written over 150 legal publications, and teaches at the University of Alberta Law School in Constitutional Litigation.

Introduction[1]

Catholic education – and, in particular, publicly funded Catholic education – is part of the heart, soul, and history of Canada. Its existence contributes to the variety, divergence, and strength of education in our country. The insistence of Catholic education on a Christ-centred, fully permeated Catholic atmosphere, based upon the whole-person development of the child, has been fundamental in the evolution and development of Canadian society.

Publicly funded Catholic education in Canada reaches as far back as the United Kingdom *Emancipation Act*, 1829.[2] Legislative protection for publicly funded Catholic education was first envisioned in 1841, with the Ontario *Common Schools Act*[3]; the *Constitution Act, 1867*[4] effected constitutional protection in Ontario and Quebec. The *Rupert's Land and North-Western Territory Order, 1870*,[5] granted similar protection for a vast tract of land in the North; the *Manitoba Act, 1870*,[6] did the same for Manitoba; and the *Alberta Act, 1905*,[7] and *Saskatchewan Act, 1905*,[8] entrenched protection in those western provinces, respectively. This paper will trace the history of Catholic education in Canada and reflect upon its current and future status.

Early Catholic Education in the Atlantic Provinces

Catholic education in Canada dates back to the first wintering of European settlers in Port Royal in 1604.[9] In the early 1800s, a number of charitable societies began delivering education in Newfoundland as an outreach to their charitable purposes. These included the Society for the Preservation of the Gospel, the Society for the Improvement for the Conditions of the

Poor, the Newfoundland School Society, and the Benevolent Irish Society. By 1802, Bishop O'Donel supported the foundation of "charity schools," and by 1826, Bishop Scallan had founded the Orphan Asylum School.

In 1830, Bishop Michael Fleming of St. John's opened the first formal Catholic school in Newfoundland, and brought the Presentation Sisters and the Sisters of Mercy to Newfoundland to staff it. The *Newfoundland Education Act* of 1836 established non-sectarian public schools in that province, and granted financial support to church schools that were in existence by that date. By 1843, the *Newfoundland Schools Act* provided for separate Catholic and Protestant schools, with the Protestant grant being divided in 1853. The teaching sisters were joined in 1848 by the Irish Franciscan Friars, and by 1880, Catholic education became available in Labrador. By 1876, the *Newfoundland Schools Act* recognized denominational Roman Catholic, Church of England, and Methodist Schools. Salvation Army schools were added in 1892, as were Seventh Day Adventist schools in 1912. All those religious congregations provided denominational education by the time Newfoundland and Labrador entered Confederation in 1949.[10]

Pre-Confederation, Catholic education in the Maritime provinces was based almost exclusively upon verbal understandings and "gentlemen's agreements" dating from the 1829 *Emancipation Act*.[11] St. Andrew's College was established in 1831 in Prince Edward Island, followed in 1855 by St. Dunstan's College, which later became a part of the University of Prince Edward Island.[12]

In New Brunswick, the first Catholic school for boys was established in 1842. In 1852, Bishop Connolly founded the Sisters of Charity to educate the poor, while inviting the Religious of the Sacred Heart to educate those who were better off. Until 1857, educational funding for these schools was granted annually in a lump sum "to provide for certain educational purposes," without specifying amounts for any particular school or purpose.[13] In 1858, the New Brunswick legislature passed the *Parish Schools Act,* which provided grants for Catholic schools, but did not recognize them as part of the public school system.

Under the *Parish Schools Act,* trustees were elected or appointed as other parish officers were. The schools established under this Act were Public, Parish, or District schools.[14] Therefore, only in locales where the majority of the population belonged to the same religion were the public schools denominational in character.[15] The 1858 Act did, however, provide grants for private Catholic schools.[16] These schools taught the doctrines of the Catholic religion and were under government inspection. Returns and an annual allowance were made from public funds for the 250 Catholic schools established under the Act.[17] By the time of Confederation, all the denominational schools received special grants, in addition to the amount authorized by law. Thus, at the time of the Union, denominational schools were recognized by the legislature and supported by public revenues.[18]

In 1871, New Brunswick passed the *Common Schools Act,* which provided for a non-sectarian system of tax-supported schools but did not allow for religious instruction in the curriculum. This Act prohibited the grant of public aid to schools in which Catholic doctrine was distinctively taught,[19] and was upheld in *Ex Parte Renaud*.[20] Prince Edward Island copied the *Common Schools Act* in 1877 in the *Davies School Act.*

Prior to the 1860s, the Catholic Church operated Catholic schools in Nova Scotia, maintaining them by small fees as well as by education grants provided through administrative arrangements worked out between the provincial authority, private religious bodies, and local education authorities.[21]

By 1864, the Nova Scotia *Act for the Encouragement of Education* set up public schools, provided for public school boards with elected trustees, and, in 1865, made school assessments compulsory. These Acts established a council of public instruction, county boards of commissioners, and local school boards with elected trustees. Provincial aid was given to encourage local schools. In 1866, a provincial system of common schools was established, and denominational schools continued to receive assistance in practice from public funds at the time of Confederation.[22] There was, however, no provision for formal recognition of the Catholic school system in the province.

Both immediately before and after Confederation, Catholic education in the Maritime provinces was tolerated, if not heavily supported. Limited public support came in the form of education grants, and there was recognition of Catholic schools, even if they were not afforded constitutional protection. Often, Catholic schools continued to operate post-Confederation with the consent of the local school board, particularly in areas of majority Catholic population, or in places where significant numbers of Catholic trustees sat on the public school board.[23]

Early Catholic Education in Quebec and Ontario

The earliest schools in Quebec, established in 1608, aimed to "[provide] for the basic educational needs of the French settlers, and were also intended to bring Christianity to the native population."[24] The Jesuit College was founded in Quebec City in 1635, later evolving into Université Laval; the religious teaching orders of the Ursulines, Recollets, Sulpicians, Frères Charon, and Congrégation de Notre-Dame were active in education in Montreal and Quebec throughout the 1600s and 1700s.

Under the *Constitution Act, 1791* (UK), the British government left Upper and Lower Canada to organize education in the new world. In turn, the governments of Upper and Lower Canada left the matter largely to the Roman Catholic, Methodist, Church of England, and Presbyterian churches.[25] This situation changed dramatically with the *Act of Union*, 1841, and the legislation following upon that Act.

Upper Canada

The *Common Schools Act* of 1841 provided that "any number of inhabitants of a different faith from the majority in such township or parish might choose their own trustees and … establish and maintain one or more common schools" on the same basis as, and receiving the same government grants as, the existing common schools. This was the first provision for denominational or separate schools in Canada, and was driven largely by the representatives of the Church of England and the Presbyterians in Upper Canada, who sought a distinct denominational education from the majority Methodists.[26]

In 1843, the Reform government of Baldwin and Lafontaine introduced *An Act for the Establishment and Maintenance of Common Schools in Upper Canada*, which established a number of fundamental principles that were to become the foundation of all subsequent separate school legislation. These included that parents had the right to determine whether their children would receive denominational education, that denominational separate schools would be state-controlled common schools, that such separate schools might be either Roman Catholic or Protestant, and that separate schools were to be subject to the same control, regulations, and rules as common schools, and were entitled to receive proportionate government grants.[27]

The most influential educational figure of the day was Dr. Egerton Ryerson, who held the office of Superintendent of Common Schools in Upper Canada and Ontario from 1844 to 1876. He recognized separate school education as "a protection of the minority against any oppressive or invidious proceedings on the part of the majority,"[28] particularly when the "strong ... and often exasperated, feelings between Irish Protestants and Roman Catholics did not permit them to unite in the school education of their children."[29]

Ryerson drafted the *Common Schools Act, 1859*,[30] which codified all of the previously existent separate school legislation under one Act; he also influenced the *Taché Act, 1855*,[31] and later the *Scott Act, 1863*,[32] which was the Act constitutionalized for the province of Ontario by section 93(1) of the *Constitution Act, 1867*.

The *Taché Act* was presented to the Upper Canada Legislature in May 1855.[33] Section II of the Act provided that "not less than five heads of families ... being Roman Catholics ... may convene a public meeting of persons desiring to establish a separate school for Roman Catholics"; section VI provided for the expansion of separate schools by union of separate school wards. It also provided the power to impose, levy, and collect school rates or subscriptions, and granted separate schools the same rights and powers possessed by common schools (s. VIII). Finally, it provided that separate school supporters would be relieved from the taxation support of common schools, and allocated an annual share in government grants for the support of separate schools on a proportionate basis (s. XIII).

The *Scott Act, 1863,* found strong support from two leading figures of Upper Canada: Sir John A. Macdonald and Thomas D'Arcy McGee.[34] It provided that any five heads of families, being Roman Catholic, could call a meeting for the establishment of a separate Catholic school, at which the supporters could elect three trustees, that the various separate school trustees "of any city or town, shall form one body corporate," and that different school sections could combine together to form a "Separate School Union Section" as a method of expanding the boundaries of separate schools. The trustees of a separate school section or union section had the duty and power to "impose, levy and collect school rates or subscriptions" for separate schools and were entitled to educate the Roman Catholic children and any "children from other School Sections, whose parents or lawful guardians are Roman Catholics, to be received into a Separate School under their management."

Separate school supporters were exempted from paying common school rates and were entitled to a pro-rata proportion of annual grants by the legislature, as well as "all other public grants, investments and allotments for Common School purposes." As part of the management of separate schools, Catholic trustees had the right to prescribe the courses of study to be taught in their school.[35] This was the status of Catholic education in Upper Canada at the time of Confederation.

Lower Canada

In Lower Canada, the first provision for denominational separate schools was established in the *Education Act, 1846*.[36] Denominational separate schools in Lower Canada were Protestant, because the majority of the population was Catholic.[37]

Montreal and Quebec City established a unique education system: in these cities, there were two elected boards of denominational school commissioners, each autonomous, and neither designated as majority or minority, public or separate. Every school in either city was under the management and control of the Board of Commissioners chosen from persons of their particular religious faith. The examination of teachers, selection of books, and right to visit the schools were based on a separation of faiths. Catholics in Montreal or Quebec City had the right to schools controlled and managed by Catholic Commissioners and staffed by Catholic teachers who were evaluated by Catholic examiners; like privileges belonged to the Protestants of each city with regard to the schools controlled by the Protestant Board of Commissioners.[38] Other rights conferred on Catholics and Protestants included the right to elect trustees of their own faith, the right of control over and the right to choose teaching staff within certain legislative limits, the exclusive right to the choice of books of religion by the ecclesiastical authorities of their denomination, the unlimited power of taxation of their co-religionists, and a discretionary power of borrowing within the limits determined by law.[39]

Outside of Quebec City and Montreal, the *Education Act, 1846*, established a system of dissentient schools, where "the inhabitants so dissentient ... signify such dissent in writing."

This provision meant that the common schools were managed by school commissioners elected by all the landowners and householders of the municipality, other than the dissentient inhabitants. Dissentient schools were maintained by trustees of the dissentient faith, and the course of study to be followed in each school was regulated by those trustees.[40] Although the *Education Act, 1846,* was amended and consolidated by the *Education Act, 1861,* "few changes in the law had been made since 1846."[41]

Early Catholic Education in Rupert's Land and the North-Western Territory

Beginning in the late 1830s, the Hudson's Bay Company determined that it would be advantageous to encourage basic education of the Native and Métis populations in Rupert's Land and the North-Western Territory, which it accomplished by supporting missionary work in the territories.

In 1838, two Oblate missionaries, Father Blanchet and Father Demurs, arrived in Fort Edmonton; in 1842, the Oblate missionary Father Thibeault founded the first permanent mission, on the shores of Lac Ste. Anne. By 1844, Oblate Father Bourassa was preaching in central and northern Alberta and working at Lac St. Anne, Lesser Slave Lake, and Grande Prairie. In 1885, Father de Smet, who travelled with the Blackfoot of central Alberta, spent time in Fort Edmonton negotiating a peace treaty between the Blackfoot and Flathead tribes. He was joined in 1853 by Father Remas. All of these missionaries mixed education with their missionary duties. However, the first permanent formal schooling in Alberta was introduced by Father Albert Lacombe at Lac Ste. Anne in 1852, and included systematized instruction of adult and young Indians and Métis.

The state of education in Rupert's Land and the North-Western Territory at this time was largely unorganized. The Privy Council in the case of *Brophy* v. *Manitoba* said: "Prior to [July 15, 1870] ... there did not exist in the territory then incorporated any public system of education. The several religious denominations had established such schools as they thought fit, and maintained them by means of funds voluntarily contributed by the members of their own communion. None of them received any state aid."[42]

Early Catholic Education in British Columbia

Catholic education on the west coast was always private in nature, due to the significant majority of Protestant English – and, later, American – settlers to the area. The Colonial Reports of Sir James Douglas dated October 27, 1849, recorded that Oblate priests were providing education to the wives and children of Hudson's Bay employees.[43] The Sisters of St. Ann founded an early private Catholic school at Fort Victoria in 1858. The need for teaching personnel grew with the arrival of the Caribou Gold Rush of 1858, and Bishop Demers recruited teaching sisters for girls from the Sisters of St. Ann, the Sisters of Our Lady of Charity, the Sisters of the Child Jesus, and the Sisters of Charity of Providence[44]; boys' schools were later established by the Oblates of Mary Immaculate and the Irish Christian Brothers.[45] By 1900, there were 25 Catholic schools in British Columbia.[46] There was no history of public support for Catholic institutions until 1907, when Catholic churches and halls were granted tax exemption, followed in later years by grants of free textbooks, limited health-care services, and school exemption from municipal property taxation.

The Constitutionalization of the Denominational School Status Quo

One of the principal issues debated by the Fathers of Confederation at the Charlottetown Conference of 1864, and later at the London Conference of 1866–1867, was the "denominational school issue."[47] This matter was of such importance that it was not merely added to the division of powers in the draft of the new constitution, but an entire constitutional section about it was added.[48] It is generally agreed that Confederation would not have been achieved in Canada without the protections accorded to denominational schools that were forged largely by D'Arcy McGee in 1864 and Alexander Galt in 1866. The most often quoted excerpt to this effect is the speech in the House of Commons of Prime Minister Sir Charles Tupper in 1896, where he said: "... but for the assent that in the Confederation Act should be embodied a clause which would protect the rights of minorities, whether Catholic or Protestant, in this country, there would have been no Confederation...."[49]

The result of the fundamental compact to which Sir Charles Tupper referred was section 93 of the *Constitution Act, 1867,* which allocated jurisdiction over education to the provinces, but prevented them from adversely affecting denominational education rights in effect at the time of Confederation.[50]

These constitutional protections are reinforced by section 29 of the Charter of Rights of Freedoms: "Nothing in this Charter abrogates or derogates from any rights or privileges guaranteed by or under the Constitution of Canada in respect of denominational, separate or dissentient schools."[51]

The Government of Canada publication *The Charter of Rights and Freedoms: A Guide for Canadians* confirms that "the establishment and operation of religious schools will not be adversely affected by any other provisions of the Charter."[52]

The *Manitoba Act, 1870*

Prior to 1870, the Catholic and Protestant religious denominations provided education in the Red River Colony and other populated portions of Manitoba. School funding was obtained from the Council of Assiniboia, the Hudson's Bay Company, sponsoring churches, and tuition fees.[53]

On February 8, 1870, the delegates of the Red River settlement, meeting in convention, "agreed to accept the invitation held out by the Canadian Government,[54] and sent a delegation to Ottawa to agree on the terms for a peaceful entry of the country into the Dominion."[55] The following day, the convention selected Father Ritchot, Alfred Scott, and Judge Black as its three representatives.[56]

The delegates travelled to Ottawa, and negotiations with Canadian representatives commenced on Monday, April 25, 1870, with "a demand for Separate Schools for Roman Catholics, supported by public money, on a basis of population...."[57]

The Province of Manitoba came into existence on July 15, 1870, the same day Rupert's Land and the North-Western Territory were admitted into the Dominion of Canada and Parliament attempted to extend the constitutional protections of the *Constitution Act, 1867*, to the new province of Manitoba.

The Rupert's Land and North-Western Territory Order, 1870

"[T]he work of nation building" had strong political support in the first Parliament, convened on November 7, 1867.[58] One of the early deeds of the new Parliament was to draft an address in which Parliament asked the Queen to extend the Dominion of Canada "westward to the shores of the Pacific Ocean."[59]

On April 9, 1869, the Hudson's Bay Company accepted "terms for the surrender of Rupert's Land" effective December 1, 1869.[60] A deed of surrender was signed on November 19, 1869. The Government of Canada passed *An Act for the Temporary Government of Rupert's Land and the North-Western Territory When United with Canada*, S.C. 1869, c. 3, which became law on June 22, 1869.[61]

The Queen, exercising jurisdiction bestowed on her by section 146 of the *Constitution Act, 1867*, through the *Rupert's Land and North-Western Territory Order*, issued on June 23, 1870, united the North-Western Territory and Rupert's Land with the Dominion of Canada.

The Riel Rebellion and the Northwest Rebellion

In 1871, the Manitoba Legislature passed the *Education Act*, which continued the denominational schooling arrangements that had existed prior to Manitoba's entry into Confederation. The Act provided for Catholic denominational schools supported by Catholic taxpayers and for Protestant denominational schools supported by Protestant taxpayers, and allowed the schools to share provincial grants proportionally, according to population.

Unfortunately, the Red River Rebellion of 1869–1870 and the Northwest Rebellion of 1885 pitted the French/Métis/

Catholic population directly against the English/Protestant population of the new province of Manitoba specifically, and against Canada in general.

Public and government anger towards the French/Métis/Catholic population became manifest in the *Public Schools Act, 1890,* passed by the Manitoba legislature of Thomas Greenway. The Act seized all Catholic denominational school facilities, transferred them to the public school system, and allocated all public funding to the public system. The legal battles resulted in two decisions of the Judicial Committee of the Privy Council: *Barrett* v. *Winnipeg (City)*[62] and *Brophy* v. *Manitoba (Attorney General).*[63] *Barrett* held that based on the educational system for the Catholic minority in 1867, the date of the Union, the 1890 legislation did not "prejudicially affect" the rights of Catholics in Manitoba. Catholics responded by petitioning the Sir John Abbott government for a remedial order requesting the restoration of Catholic education denominational rights. The Abbott government referred the issue to the Supreme Court of Canada, which further referred the question to the Privy Council in London, England. The *Brophy* decision held that Catholics had a right of appeal to the federal government in respect of rights and privileges granted by the *Education Act, 1871.* The Privy Council indicated that at the date of the Union, and prior to the *Manitoba Act, 1870,* the Roman Catholic minority controlled and managed their own schools in the Red River Colony, although they did not receive state aid in terms of grants, there being no formal state in the Red River Colony prior to 1870; they did enjoy assessments levied upon their own faith for the denominational schooling of their children.

As a result, in 1895, the Mackenzie Bowell government passed an order directing the Province of Manitoba to return denominational rights and privileges to the Catholic population of that province. The Thomas Greenway government of Manitoba refused to pass this legislation. In 1896, Sir Wilfrid Laurier, the new prime minister, met with Premier Greenway and reached a political compromise that allowed limited Catholic religious instruction in the public schools, but only during restrictive hours; employment of Catholic teachers in the public school system; and instruction in French, though again under very restrictive conditions. The compromise did not allow for privately established Catholic schools to share in public funding, while Catholic ratepayers were still required to support the public school system.[64]

The late 19th-century education debacle in Manitoba was central to the development of denominational educational provisions in Alberta and Saskatchewan. During the formation of the two new provinces, Prime Minister Laurier was firmly resolved to avoid the crisis that had beset Manitoba and had deprived the minority Catholic, francophone, and Métis population of effective denominational education.

The Northwest Territories

On June 23, 1870, based upon *An Act for the Temporary Government of Rupert's Land and the North-Western Territory When United with Canada*,[65] *An Order of Her Majesty in Council Admitting Rupert's Land and the North-western Territory into the Union*,[66] and *An Act to Make Further Provision for the Government of the North West Territories*, the federal government passed the first *North-West Territories Act, 1875*, which provided that "the minority of the rate-payers ..., whether Protestant or Roman Catholic, may establish separate schools ..., and that ... the rate-payers establishing such Protestant or Roman Catholic separate schools shall be liable only to assessments of such rates as they may impose upon themselves in respect thereof."[67]

This Act specifically identified the rights of those of the religious majority, whether Protestant or Catholic, to establish a public school district, while allowing a religious minority, whether Protestant or Catholic, to establish a separate school district. This provision, which has since been repeatedly affirmed through legislation and court decisions at both the provincial and federal levels, formed the basis for the system of public and separate schooling in what is now Alberta and Saskatchewan.

The important codification of this education right, because of its eventual constitutionalization by virtue of the *School Ordinance, 1901*, was s. 14 of the *North-West Territories Act*, which reaffirmed that "the minority of the ratepayers …, whether Protestant or Roman Catholic, may establish separate schools."[68]

Alberta and Saskatchewan

By 1905, the Manitoba Attorney General and Minister of Education, Sir Clifford Sifton, had left Manitoba provincial politics and was sitting as the Laurier government's Minister of the Interior. Supported by Sir Frederick Haultain, Premier of the Northwest Territories, and David Goggin, Superintendent of Education for the territories, Sifton strongly advocated a single public "national school system" for the new provinces of Alberta and Saskatchewan. This non-religious system was "designed to inculcate a common set of 'national' (i.e. British/Canadian) values."[69] At the same time, Wilfrid Laurier had made a commitment to the French and Catholic populations of Quebec and Manitoba not to repeat the errors of the

Manitoba Act, 1870, and to ensure a system of viable separate schools in the new provinces similar to that in Ontario.

On February 21, 1905, Laurier introduced the first draft of the Autonomy Bills in the House of Commons. The school provisions of those Bills sparked a controversy that is commonly called the "North-West Schools Question"; it resulted in Sifton's resignation from Cabinet and brought the Laurier government to the brink of collapse.

In the first reading of the Bills, there was no reference to the separate school provisions of the *Ordinances of the Northwest Territories, 1901*. Instead, the denominational education protections were to be those "in continuance of the principles heretofore sanctioned under the *Northwest Territories Act, 1875.*" Sifton argued that this clause would have "(1) allowed the minority faiths in the new provinces to reclaim the full range of rights and privileges that were laid out in the 1875 legislation, and that had been enjoyed by religious minorities prior to 1892; (2) given those minority faith rights as enunciated in 1875 the full protection of s. 93 of the *British North America Act* – in other words the 1875 provisions would have been entrenched in the constitutions of the two new provinces."[70]

On March 8, 1905, Laurier appointed Justice Minister Sir Charles Fitzpatrick to address the education crisis. Fitzpatrick, an Irish Catholic lawyer, had been defence counsel for Louis Riel on his charge of treason against the federal government in 1885. (Later, Fitzpatrick would become Chief Justice of Canada, participating in the first Supreme Court of Canada case to interpret separate school rights in the new provinces in the case of *Regina Public School District v. Grattan Separate School District*.[71]) In the meantime, Sifton,

Frank Oliver (owner of the *Edmonton Bulletin*), J.G. Turriff, Walter Scott, and Thomas Greenway (the former premier of Manitoba) proposed to constitutionalize the status quo with respect to separate schools as reflected in the *Ordinances of the Northwest Territories, 1901*. This proposal, with the addition of the Lamont Amendment, allowing religious instruction in both the public and separate schools in the new provinces, eventually passed the House of Commons on July 20, 1905.

Laurier and Sifton both considered the final version of the education provisions to be a compromise. Sifton is reported to have characterized a failure to reach such a compromise as potentially leading to "a complete smash-up followed by dissolution and a recasting of the parties on religious and racial lines."[72]

In explaining the compromise, Liberal MP Walter Scott said that "it would simply be going beyond all reason to expect Laurier to induce Quebec to swallow a third time ... after Catholics have lost separate school rights in Manitoba, and Quebec had to accept the sending of Canadian troops to South Africa in 1899."[73]

According to David Bercuson, "The meaning of the vote held in the Commons at the end of the exhaustive debate stretching out over more than three months is clear; s. 17(1) of the *Alberta Act of 1905* would perpetuate the rights and powers of separate school boards as enunciated in Chapters 29 and 30 of the 1901 Territorial Ordinances, and no one but a hermit could have thought otherwise."[74]

The final version of s. 17 of the *Alberta Act, 1905*, and the *Saskatchewan Act, 1905*, provided that section 93 of *The British North America Act, 1867*, would apply to those provinces, but that nothing in any education law could prejudicially affect any right or privilege with respect to separate schools or with respect to religious instruction in any public or separate school as provided for in the 1901 Ordinances.

The Territorial Experience

Catholic schools were first established in the Yukon during the time of the Klondike gold rush. Later, the *Yukon Act, 1898,* entrenched Catholic rights and privileges, including education. Currently, Yukon Catholic schools are subject to the *Yukon Education Act*[75] and follow a program of studies set by the British Columbia Minister of Education and the Canadian Conference of Catholic Bishops–approved religious education program. Catholic schools are fully funded, and today three Catholic schools operate in the Whitehorse area. Three attempts by British Columbia to annex the Yukon – in 1905, 1912, and 1937 – were frustrated by separate school rights for persons of the minority denomination, Roman Catholic or Protestant, in the Yukon.[76]

In the Northwest Territories, as in Alberta and Saskatchewan, Catholic education rights may be traced to the *North-West Territories Act, 1875*,[77] the *North-West Territories Act, 1880*,[78] and the *Ordinances of the North-West Territories, 1901*. Those provisions, however, did not become constitutionalized in the Northwest Territories as they did in Alberta and Saskatchewan, and remain territorial legislation. Therefore, they are not protected by section 93(1) of the *Constitution Act, 1867*.[79] The first Catholic school system was established in Yellowknife in 1951, followed by St. Patrick's Elementary School in 1953. St. Patrick's is now a high school, and has been joined by three other schools: St. Joseph and Weledeh Catholic schools, and more recently the Kimberlite Career & Technical Centre. In total, the three schools educate 42 percent of the student population of the Northwest Territories.[80]

The Loss of Publicly Funded Catholic Education in Quebec and Newfoundland/Labrador

While publicly funded Catholic education has continued to strengthen and expand in Ontario, Saskatchewan, Alberta, and the North, it has been lost in Quebec and Newfoundland and Labrador.

In Quebec, the change began in 1982 with the introduction of legislation for linguistically based school boards, a change to which the Quebec bishops gave assent.[81] Despite numerous legal challenges, the Supreme Court of Canada ultimately ruled that the proposed legislation "did not prejudicially affect school rights of minorities and did not offend section 93 of the *British North America Act*."[82] By 1989, Bill 107 provided for a linguistically based school system, recognizing the rights of Catholics and Protestants in the confessional schools of Montreal and Quebec and the dissentient boards outside of those two cities.[83] By April 1997, the Quebec National Assembly had determined to ask for an amendment to the *Constitution Act, 1867*, to exclude Quebec from denominational education protections. The Act was approved by the National Assembly and the federal government in late 1997, and Quebec was exempted from the constitutional protections. In 1999, a provincially appointed task force resulted in the passage of Bill 118 in 2000, and the confessional status of publicly supported Catholic education was repealed. To reduce the potential for a constitutional challenge, the National Assembly invoked the notwithstanding clause of the *Constitution Act, 1982*, and "the secularization of the Quebec school system was complete."[84]

The beginning of the end of publicly funded Catholic education in Newfoundland and Labrador started with the Royal Commission Report of 1992, which included "recommendations that pertained to having the churches give up the exercise of their constitutional rights in education."[85]

A referendum was held on September 5, 1995, for the establishment of a single publicly funded education system, which carried by a 10 percent margin. This resulted in an amendment to Newfoundland and Labrador's constitution, which "made the implementation … legislatively and practically cumbersome." When several school boards chose to ignore the results of Newfoundland's "preference process," the Newfoundland Supreme Court issued an injunction against the closure of Catholic schools except with the consent of Catholic school representatives.[86] The result was a second referendum, held on September 2, 1997, which allowed the constitutional protection to be completely rewritten so as to eradicate publicly funded Catholic schools in the province, prevented the teaching of denominational religious programs in public schools, and provided for a government-drafted religious education program. "Consequently, as of September, 1998, there are no publicly funded Roman Catholic schools in Newfoundland."[87]

The Expansion of Catholic Education in British Columbia, Alberta, and Ontario

Catholic education in British Columbia, although not based upon a constitutional foundation, has seen a considerable improvement in the last half-century. By registering under the

Societies Act in 1957, Catholic schools were able to have their properties exempted from taxation, and in 1977 the *British Columbia Independent Schools Support Act* made student grants available to qualifying Catholic schools at 30 percent of the per student costs of the local public school districts. In 1989, the *Independent School Act* raised that grant to 50 percent of the per student operating cost of public schools.[88]

In Alberta, a series of court victories through the 1980s and 1990s provided Catholic schools with funding equitable to what their public counterparts received.[89] This occurred through the expansion of the tax assessment base available to these Catholic schools and by government grants. In 1994, the Alberta government passed the *School Amendment Act, 1994*, which allowed separate Catholic schools to continue to access their own assessment base, and then be topped up to the total per pupil amount from general revenues. In this way, Catholic schools were entitled to parity with their public counterparts, but were still enabled to access their own assessment base without penalty or deprivation of the traditional constitutional rights of Catholic school supporters. This system of funding was approved by the Supreme Court of Canada in *Public School Boards Association of Alberta* v. *Alberta (Attorney General)*.[90]

In Ontario, a significant change in policy occurred in 1984 with the recognition of publicly funded secondary schools.[91] In 1995, the Royal Commission on Learning report rescinded the legislative clause preventing Catholic boards from preferring Catholic teachers at the secondary level. In 1997, the Ontario government proposed a new funding model that "would provide equitable funding for all school boards, whether public or Catholic, urban or rural," but "the right to levy taxes would be held in abeyance."[92] In March 2001, the Supreme Court of Canada ruled in *Ontario English Catholic Teachers Assn. v. Ontario (Attorney General)*[93] that Catholic schools in Ontario were entitled to receive equitable financial support through provincial grants, not based on assessments of supporters of the Catholic boards.

Into the Future

Catholic education has been with us since the earliest European settlements in North America, first in the form of missionary instruction, and later in the context of formal education, whether publicly or privately funded. The ebb and flow of Catholic rights has substantially stabilized in Ontario, Alberta, and Saskatchewan by constitutional protection, and in the Yukon and Northwest Territories by territorial legislation. In these jurisdictions, Catholic education stands on an essentially equal footing with public education. On the other hand, publicly funded Catholic education has been lost in the past few decades in Quebec and in Newfoundland and Labrador. The status of Catholic education in those provinces is now on the same footing as in the Maritime provinces, Manitoba, and British Columbia, where Catholic education is private, with limited provincial support in some jurisdictions.

Whatever the level of legislative protection or public funding, though, Catholic education remains alive and well in all of the provinces and territories in Canada, which is a testament to Catholic parents' desire and efforts for a comprehensive education system based upon gospel values that develops their children intellectually, physically, emotionally, and spiritually.

Chapter 4

FROM THE GATES OF THE NEW JERUSALEM TO THE TASTE OF ASHES: REFLECTIONS ON POLITICAL ACTIVISM AND FAITH

Peter Warrian

Peter Warrian was elected president of the Canadian Union of Students in 1968. He served as Canadian Research Director of the United Steelworkers of America and as the chief economist of Bob Rae's NDP government in Ontario. Born and raised in Toronto, he is currently a Senior Research Fellow at the Munk School of Global Affairs at the University of Toronto and a member of the Board of Governors of Regis College.

My life in activism began when I joined a Toronto student chapter of the Catholic Workers movement in the early 1960s. It was not surprising that 30 years later I was the chief economist of a New Democratic Party (NDP) government. However, the path that led there was anything but a straight line. My political activism and spiritual life were grounded in the Dorothy Day wing of Catholicism.

Twice in my activist life, I thought the movement had gotten to at least the Gates of the New Jerusalem: first, at the apex of the protest against the war in Vietnam, when United States president Richard Nixon announced American withdrawal; and second, with the election of Bob Rae's NDP government in Ontario in 1990. In both cases, the vision of the Holy City crumbled, and activists were left not with the fruits of victory but with the taste of ashes. The experience shakes you to your spiritual core.

The Beginnings

I grew up in a working-class household in suburban Toronto. Our family's politics were mildly Liberal. Red Kelly was both captain of the Maple Leafs and our Member of Parliament.

My first step into politics and political engagement came when a high school buddy of mine and I drove to Rochester during the 1964 race riots. We were political spectators. That experience, plus the idealism of John F. Kennedy, led me to connect with other Catholic high schoolers. I attended a public high school, and came into casual contact with some people who were organizing a student chapter of the Catholic Workers.

Catholic Social Teaching

The Catholic Worker Bible was comprised of the great 20th-century Catholic social teachings: *Rerum Novarum*, *Quadragesima Anno*, and *Pacem in Terris*. The background display of Vatican II was matched in our foreground with trade union rights and the civil rights movement. Martin Luther King was not the only speaker that famous day in Washington. So was Walter Reuther of the United Auto Workers. I wasn't there, but I watched it on television.

At Ivan Illich's Center in Cuernavaca, Mexico, I met veteran Catholic members of the various movements struggling for justice and political change in Latin America. It taught me that revolution – real revolution – almost always takes place in contexts of war and famine. I learned not to use the word loosely. I also learned not to romanticize political violence.

The Gates of the New Jerusalem I

It is probably true to say that for young Catholic activists in 1968, Vatican II and Woodstock were virtually indistinguishable. We were all marching down the same road to the same ethical and social horizon.

Later, as things started to come unstuck, political ideology came to dominate. There was a strong tendency to romanticize violence as a political means, and a naive assumption that identity politics was inherently progressive. We never dreamed of Kosovo.

Entering the '60s movement, religion was accepted as a common intellectual and spiritual background for all the activists I knew and worked with. The Catholic Worker movement started the anti-Vietnam protest: two lonely pickets in front of the United Nations building in New York in 1961. The peace movement was filled with activists from the student Christian movement.

After 1968, in my experience, ideological identities came more and more to the fore, and religious identities were marginalized. If anything, spirituality came to be associated with the drug culture and withdrawal from politics.

The Aftermath

In my experience, my friends – most of whom were student activists in the aftermath of the failure of the 68ers – withdrew from activism into private life: rural communes, professional careers, sometimes drugs. However, a not insignificant number of student leaders went into the labour movement and had a major effect on trade union strategies and policies in Canada.

The Gates of the New Jerusalem II

When I joined the labour movement in the 1970s, there was a real movement with overall social and political, mostly social democratic, objectives. Today there are still unions and collective bargaining, which are much needed in an era of globalization and the declining living standards of the middle classes. But there is not a labour movement in the more profound sense of when I signed up.

Canada was fairly unique in the number of former student activists who became active in the leadership as well as senior staff in the labour movement in Canada. This had an important impact on the economic and social policy formulations of the labour movement, as it became much more nationalistic and interventionist than most of the postwar trade union platform, in contrast to directions in the U.S. movement.

The central issues motivating people were redistribution, economic justice, and improved living standards, health care, and education for all. For better or for worse, under our labour laws, unions do not bargain with the economy; they bargain with individual employers for specified groups of workers. Their very success has been their potential downfall. A labour convention is not comprised of those most in need; it represents the relatively well-off middle class. Steelworkers work in mills but drive SUVs. That was so, at least until the 2008 Great Recession, which has seen hard-won wages and benefits rolled back by economic forces, a renewed right-wing austerity movement, and the external threat of China.

In fact, labour conventions are mostly dominated now by public sector union members. The almost unbroken upward trend in public sector wages and benefits has produced the unsustainable result of group privilege where the politics of resentment (e.g., public sector unions fighting against co-payment of pension liabilities while 75 percent of people have no personal pension) has created an ugly prospect. "Labour struggle" and "working class" are no longer closely correlated.

Activists in Power: The NDP Government

Theoretically, the achievement of an NDP/social democratic government in power should be the opportunity to consolidate and advance gains for workers, as well as to substantially extend collective bargaining achievements to all working people. That was the history of Medicare in Canada and the history of public pensions. It is a noble history.

Unfortunately, my experience in government was not a coalescing of the movement and extension of labour gains to all. It was more a cruel lesson in the amplification of divisions in the labour and social movements. There was and is no unified social and economic program of the left. Gaps between the private sector and industrial unions on the one side and the public sector unions on the other were unbreachable. There was no near-term mechanism for extending wage and benefit gains achieved in the organized sector to the broader working-class base. There was no way politically to balance budgetary allocations between daycare, for instance, and reinvestment needs for infrastructure and new technologies to boost productivity in ways that would make the economic redistributions more sustainable in the long term.

The Rae government's noble failure in the 'social contract' attempt to bridge these gaps proved too wide for existing political means and the NDP's political horizon. It was a debacle and defeat for all, but the inevitable blame fell on the government alone. It was we who were in the government who deservedly took the first lash, but in the end the inability of the broader labour and social movement to acknowledge and accept co-responsibility has disarmed forward progress ever since. No one could answer the question "So what did you learn from the NDP's time in government?" The echo in the room says it all.

The Aftermath

The result was a one-sided descent into accusation and recrimination, mostly in the labour movement but also across other social movements. The left has never recovered from this hole in its core discourse. What it most lacked was a conversation about shared values. In fact, values-based discernment became even scarcer. Activists dug deeper into the cul-de-sac of single-issue campaigns. More aggressive secularism questioned the legitimacy of religion and religious values in the public square.

I said to friends that the best preparation for a life of prayer is to be chief economist of an NDP government. It tasted like ashes. (This phrase comes from Marci Shore's book *The Taste of Ashes: The Afterlife of Totalitarianism in Eastern Europe*. She writes about the life of the Eastern European Jewish Marxist intelligentsia under Stalinism. They couldn't *not* believe.)

My religious beliefs had constrained my engagement with the drug culture after 1968. It similarly constrained my engagement with the blame game after the NDP debacle. Obviously, something else was going on politically behind the scenes during the torturous social contract process. However, I declined multiple requests to write the whistleblower book and name names. The level of denial about mutual failure among the NDP leadership, trade union leaders, and social movement activists made any constructive debate impossible. I didn't want to make the left feel any worse about itself than it already did.

The Taste of Ashes

The Gates of the New Jerusalem drifted further away. The experience of the Rae government, I think, exhausted most of my generation's political energy and will towards qualitative social change. It was the worst feeling in the world, even worse than the post-Vietnam withdrawal into private life. This was a collective defeat and eclipse of a shared ethical and social horizon.

In a completely out-of-character moment for me, I found a base for spiritual regeneration by going to the movies: *The Lord of the Rings*, Peter Jackson's adaptation of Tolkien's trilogy. It is basically the Gospel according to St. John.

John's Gospel has never been a favourite on the playlist of Catholic social activists. At its core, the Gospel takes the position that we do not build the kingdom; God does. Remember Gandalf's instruction to Frodo: "The Lord of the Rings does not share power. We do not make the times. It is only what we do with the times we are given."

The other major lesson from the movie, for me, was how it instructs us on the voice with which the Church can speak to the world. It is an inclusive voice, telling a universal story with minimal use of traditional religious symbols and language.

From Cataphatic to Apophatic Spirituality

From the days of the student movement, the labour movement, and the NDP government, I have been associated with the urban myth that I was a Jesuit. It was not the case biographically, but may be true in some way in character. My real direct engagement with the Jesuits came only in the last 10 years.

It was by doing the Ignatian Spiritual Exercises that I re-architected my spirituality for the times. Someone with a Dorothy Day Catholic Worker / student activist / trade union life history for 40 years has an ironclad engagement in a cataphatic spirituality: that is, to see and strive to achieve God's work directly in the world. Build the kingdom in those economic and social ways that are most available and appropriate. That was me.

The shift, perhaps related to age but also after reflecting on the taste of ashes, was to a different kind of spirituality. An apophatic spirituality is a 'negative' theology, focusing instead on mystery and the limits of language.

It is not finished. But it feels right and comfortable in relating to others in the world. As philosopher Charles Taylor says, the believer and non-believer share a common project and agenda confronting society and political efficacy in our globalized and cynical world: What is the basis for social solidarity? What is the basis for civic engagement?

This we share. So would Dorothy Day.

Chapter 5

FAITH AND POLITICS: REFLECTIONS FROM THE FRONT LINE

John Milloy

John Milloy is a former Ontario Provincial Cabinet Minister who served as Member of Provincial Parliament for Kitchener Centre from 2003 to 2014. Prior to that, he worked on Parliament Hill in Ottawa, including five years in the Office of Prime Minister Jean Chrétien, where he served as Legislative Assistant. He is currently the co-director of the Centre for Public Ethics and assistant professor of public ethics at Waterloo Lutheran Seminary, and the inaugural practitioner in residence in Wilfrid Laurier University's political science department. He is also a lecturer in the Master of Public Service program at the University of Waterloo.

He holds a doctorate in modern history from Oxford University and an M.A. in international history from the London School of Economics.

Can a person of faith succeed in public office and remain true to their religious beliefs? How should persons of faith approach voting and participation in civic life? How can faith communities influence political decision-making? Such questions are not academic. They are both practical and relevant to a modern pluralistic society.

I am a practising Catholic who has spent most of the last 20 years as a senior adviser on Parliament Hill and an elected representative and cabinet minister in Ontario. In these roles I refused to check my faith at the door. I struggled, I compromised, and I stumbled, but I never filed my faith away as a personal matter unrelated to my political activities. The tenets of Catholicism are clear. Catholics are called to participate fully in public life. They are also warned not to compartmentalize their beliefs into public and private spheres. In other words, if you elect a practising Roman Catholic to public office, their faith comes with them.[1]

This seems obvious. Faith helps define who you are and shapes your world-view. I was one of the longest-serving members of the provincial cabinet's Poverty Reduction Committee and was honoured to have served as Ontario's Minister of Community and Social Services, albeit during a tumultuous period. Christ's call to reach out to the vulnerable was an aspect of my faith that drove me to these issues.

Faith and Politics in Canada: The Current Situation

It is difficult to know how common my views are within the Canadian political system. I rarely heard a substantive discussion of religious faith in political circles. That does not mean that religion is not acknowledged. Politicians continue to be scrupulous in voicing their respect for faith traditions.

Meetings are postponed or cancelled because they conflict with a particular religious holy day. Representatives of various faiths are frequently asked to begin political events with a prayer or words of devotion. Preference is often given to lesser-known religions, such as those of our Indigenous peoples, to demonstrate inclusivity.

This outpouring of respect seems to end when it comes to the substance of religious belief. Religion is often caricatured as being made up of rigid, conservative, and exclusionary rules based upon supernatural revelation; rules that are overly focused on sexuality and reproduction, and out of step with the times. 'Separation of church and state' is the handy motto used privately by politicians, followed by the observation that no one has the right to impose their beliefs on others.

Obviously, governments should never favour a particular faith tradition. But don't be fooled. Politics is all about imposing a particular set of beliefs on society – beliefs that are considered better than those proposed by opposing parties. There should be nothing threatening about the fact that my faith has helped inform my political beliefs. No one comes to politics from a position of neutrality. Our experiences, upbringing, education, and familiarity with both success and failure shape our response to the challenges of the day. In fact, politicians love to talk about what motivates them. Some describe having been raised in poverty and wanting to relieve others of that hardship. Others speak of witnessing a particular injustice that drove them into politics, or wanting to improve society for their children or grandchildren.

Faith as a Factor in Entering Politics

The list of factors motivating someone to enter politics seems to stop abruptly when it comes to religious belief. This is unfortunate when you consider the nature of the problems facing our country. Many of them stem from our society's inherent selfishness and resulting reluctance to act collectively. Higher taxes may be needed to support the poor. Economic growth might need to be curbed to support environmental ends. Strangers may need to be welcomed into our community in the form of refugees fleeing war-torn lands. So many issues require all of us to be active, responsible, and engaged, yet the attitude of too many voters is 'leave me alone.'

Instead of challenging us, politicians tend to pander by promising everything to everyone and claiming there will be minimal costs. 'Sacrifice' appears to have been banned from political vocabulary, despite the fact that the solution to so many of our problems hinges on all of us contributing.

It is here that the teachings of so many faith traditions can make such a substantial contribution. As Vatican II taught us, for example,

> Profound and rapid changes make it particularly urgent that no one, ignoring the trend of events or drugged by laziness, content himself with a merely individualistic morality. It grows increasingly true that the obligations of justice and love are fulfilled only if each person, contributing to the common good, according to his own abilities and the needs of others, also promotes and assists the public and private institutions dedicated to bettering the conditions of human life ... Let everyone consider it his sacred obligation to count social necessities among the primary duties of modern man, and to pay heed to them.[2]

Stability in a Shifting Political World

Politics is messy and complicated. Problems grow more complex and resources continue to shrink. Politicians inhabit a world where their actions and even their personal lives are placed under a microscope by a 24-hour media cycle dominated by a "gotcha!" approach to news reporting. Mistakes are rarely tolerated and the electorate has grown increasingly impatient for quick action, no matter what the circumstances.

Political representatives are buffeted by a variety of forces: public opinion (sometimes of the knee-jerk variety), special interest groups, influential business and opinion leaders, financial donors, and the media. And despite the fact that politicians spend so much energy trying to be liked, the public continues to hold them in low regard.

Within this messy world is the constant need to achieve and hold on to power. "Yes, we must make compromises," it is argued, "and sometimes go close to the line, but if we don't, the other guys will win and do irreparable harm." While I was in government, it became a given that during any high-level political discussion, someone would remark that they were so glad "we" were dealing with this issue, rather than the other side.

I left politics with a list of significant achievements, and I accept that to get there often required compromise. But I also witnessed a kind of groupthink develop within all political parties. I saw a willingness to appeal to public selfishness and consumerism. Decisions were sometimes based on political expediency rather than well-thought-out policies, because winning needed to come first. And I saw each party attack other parties with viciousness and, at times, unfairness, based on the double justification that "they were doing the same thing" and if we didn't, "they might win and destroy everything we had built."

Many dangers lurk within such a world. The anchor line gets frayed and the lack of clarity of purpose can create a sense of being adrift. Winning begins to usurp everything else. At times you find yourself believing that you are always right and the other side is always wrong, while not being entirely sure what either side really stands for.

My religious beliefs helped me navigate this topsy-turvy world. Indeed, the Catholic tradition recognizes how easy it is to get lost in these turbulent times. As John Paul II commented in his encyclical *Veritatis Splendor*,

> Pilate's question "What is truth" reflects the distressing perplexity of a man who often no longer knows *who he is, whence* he comes and *where* he is going … In a positive way, the Church seeks, with great love, to help all the faithful to form a moral conscience which will make judgments and lead to decisions in accordance with the truth, following the exhortation of the Apostle Paul: "Do not be conformed to this world but be transformed by the renewal of your mind, that you may prove what is the will of God, what is good and acceptable and perfect" (*Rom* 12:2).[3]

Faith and Politics: A Personal Experience

Despite my belief in the value of my religion, "I am supportive" or "I oppose" a particular policy "because of my religious beliefs" were words I rarely used publicly at Queen's Park. A review of Hansard finds only two occasions where I spoke about the link between my religious beliefs and specific policy issues in the Legislature. One was my support for a

Private Member's Bill to create a Pope John Paul II day in the Province of Ontario. Although it was not a matter of grave public policy, I did associate my support for the Bill with my status as a practising Catholic.

The second was more substantive. In a speech to the Legislature in support of a Bill strengthening labour standards for workers, I made brief mention of Catholics in public life based on a conference I had recently attended. I noted that Catholic morality was about more than a few hot-button issues. In fact, it directly related to the rights of workers, and the values behind this legislation were consistent with my Catholic values – and, indeed, the values of all religions.

When I speak of values in a political context, I don't simply mean the recognition of what is 'good' or 'bad.' Pretty much everyone is against crime, and it would be unusual to hear a politician praising litter. The real question is priorities. How seriously would a political party in office fight to protect the environment? Would it deny a permit to establish a new factory and the jobs that accompanied it if that factory also posed an environmental threat? If a government is entering a period of austerity, how far will it go to protect the poor and vulnerable from budget cuts? The answers to these types of questions reflect the real values politicians hold.

Hot-button Issues

It is impossible to discuss the hesitancy of politicians, particularly Catholic ones, to talk about their faith publicly without mentioning the Catholic Church's stand on a number of controversial issues related to reproduction and sexuality: first and foremost, abortion, and to a lesser extent, the rights of the lesbian, gay, bisexual, transgender, queer (LGBTQ) community.

When it comes to LGBTQ rights, I have always used as a guide the Church's teaching against discrimination in this area. The *Catechism of the Catholic Church* makes clear that when it comes to gay men and women, "every sign of unjust discrimination in their regard should be avoided."[4] As a result, I have never had any hesitation when it came to supporting measures to ensure full respect for all persons, regardless of sexual orientation, and celebrating the diversity of our society.

The issue of abortion has been far more prevalent as a political issue tied to the Catholic faith. I understand the Church's strong anti-abortion position, and as a practising Roman Catholic, it is difficult to imagine a situation where I would encourage a woman to have an abortion. I become perplexed, however, when the issue moves from one of personal choice into the realm of public policy.

As a former politician – and considering the current social and political climate – I have no idea how an absolute pro-life position could realistically be translated into practical public policy that would curb abortions and find the broad acceptance needed to become law. As someone who has participated in the very complicated world of drafting laws, it is mind-boggling to think of tackling questions about regulation, penalties, and the prevention of illegal procedures within the greater context of the competing rights of the mother and the unborn child. Beyond these difficulties are the huge questions around how government and society would provide meaningful support to children born in difficult circumstances as well as to their mothers and other family members. No mainline political party has expressed any interest in opening up this issue, and as an elected official I directed my energies elsewhere, understanding that creating a more supportive society also played a role in decreasing the need for abortion.

This does not mean that I want the conversation to stop. And if I ever ran for political office again, I would refuse to commit in advance, as the leader of the federal branch of my party has demanded, to never vote for any measure that curbed abortion. The Church has a legitimate role to play in challenging conventional wisdom on this matter. What I don't understand is the Church's obsessiveness on this issue – a focus that continues to crowd out thoughtful and dynamic positions on a variety of other extremely important issues that *are* part of the current political agenda: issues such as poverty and worker's rights, the fair treatment of immigrants and refugees, international peace and security, the rights of Indigenous peoples, human trafficking, and the protection of the environment.[5] It is no surprise that Pope Francis' plea that it is not necessary to talk about "issues related to abortion, gay marriage and the use of contraceptive methods ... all the time" was welcomed so warmly by many Roman Catholics.[6]

Faith and Voting

During my third election campaign, a supporter invited me to join him for Sunday mass at his parish and the coffee hour that followed. As I made my way down to the coffee, an older woman confronted me. She proceeded to tell me that there was a group of people in the church who wanted to vote for me because I was a fellow Catholic and a "good family man." They could not do so, however, because I was a member of a political party that took positions on a number of issues, particularly abortion, that went against Church teaching.

Such a confrontation is never pleasant, and it left me a bit shaken. It raises the question, however, of how one's faith should influence how one votes. My Catholicism is much broader than one or two hot-button issues that are not part of any party's political agenda. My faith is about a set of principles that focus on protecting the poor and vulnerable, striving for equality and justice, and preserving our environment. As a Roman Catholic, I want to vote for a politician and political party that truly reflect those values in both word and action.

Several years after my encounter with this woman, the Federal Court of Canada issued a scathing attack on a policy of the federal Conservative government that denied medical coverage to refugee claimants in certain situations. Pulling no punches, and paying special attention to the innocent children of the refugee claimants involved, the court ruled that the measure could "potentially jeopardize the health, the safety and indeed the very lives of these innocent and vulnerable children in a manner that shocks the conscience and outrages our standards of decency."[7] I often wonder whether the woman I spoke to at the parish years ago ever confronted Roman Catholic federal Conservative politicians and asked them to justify their support for this policy in light of their faith.

Although as Catholics we must avoid compartmentalizing our belief system into public and private spheres, there is no clear Catholic blueprint for the appropriate role that the state should play in governing individual actions. Few would call for the banning of adultery in this day and age, although it was the subject of legal sanction in the not-too-distant past. We live in a democracy, and policy makers must recognize and respect the wide range of moral codes and activities that exist in our society.

The Doctrinal Note *On Some Questions Regarding the Participation of Catholics in Political Life*, prepared under Pope John Paul II, makes this point clear:

> Christian faith has never presumed to impose a rigid framework on social and political questions, conscious that the historical dimension requires men and women to live in imperfect situations, which are also susceptible to rapid change. For this reason, Christians must reject political positions and activities inspired by a utopian perspective.[8]

There is nothing simple or straightforward about the political process. Elected officials rarely face black-and-white situations. Politics is a world of compromise, where moving the yardstick a few centimetres towards a stated goal may be all that can be achieved. All politicians struggle with the question of how to apply their personal values to complex situations. Here again, the Catholic Church recognizes the absence of ready-made answers. As Vatican II concluded:

> Laymen should also know that it is generally the function of their well-formed Christian conscience to see that the divine law is inscribed in the life of the earthly city. From priests they look for spiritual light and nourishment. Let the layman not imagine that his pastors are always such experts, that to every problem which arises, however complicated, they can readily give him a concrete solution, or even that such is their mission. Rather, enlightened by Christian wisdom and giving close attention to the teaching authority of the Church, let the layman take on his own distinctive role.[9]

In playing their "own distinctive role", it is wrong for those on the political scene to try to "appropriate the church's authority" for their position. Catholic teaching recognizes that it is perfectly legitimate for persons of faith to disagree on a particular policy decision, and it is not the Church's role to choose sides.[10] As mentioned earlier, one of the important roles that religion plays in our society is placing itself on the outside and challenging conventional wisdom.

Faith Communities and Political Action

Although faith communities need to stay outside the political fray, they do have a role in influencing public policy and even entering into partnerships with governments on specific initiatives. As a politician, I was impressed with the number of religious groups and individuals motivated by their faith who engaged the government on concrete issues – groups like the Interfaith Social Assistance Reform Coalition (ISARC), which holds regular dialogues on poverty at Queen's Park. The Catholic Women's League was another presence at the Legislature, lobbying political representatives on a wide variety of issues. I also often met with constituents who freely associated their advocacy for issues like poverty, racism, and the plight of refugees with their religious faith.

Faith communities have remarkable power in our society. They represent thousands of members and, unlike many others who lobby government, are not motivated by self-interest. Where they fail, however, is becoming so focused on an issue where there is no common ground or room for compromise (abortion, for example) that dialogue and engagement in other areas becomes impossible.

They also tend to fall into the trap, common to so many interest groups, of refusing to acknowledge the incremental progress that is such a part of politics today. Politics truly is the art of the possible. The best that can usually be done is to take a few small steps in the right direction. At other times, particularly during periods of austerity, the best approach may be to prevent past achievements from being undone. Advocates do their cause harm when they fail to acknowledge progress, no matter how small, and instead loudly proclaim that the government has failed. Not only does this sour a constructive relationship, it makes it harder for those inside government to advocate for a cause. There is a natural reluctance to spend precious resources on initiatives that are only going to result in criticism.

Conclusion

Anyone who has held public office will tell you how overwhelming it quickly becomes. The problems facing our society are immense, and there are few solutions. We need good, thoughtful people in public life with strong values who can withstand the challenges of modern-day politics. This should include persons of all faith perspectives, including those with no religious beliefs.

Although politics is part of the secular world, faith communities and their members need to be part of the conversation. The values and perspectives that they bring to political discourse can make a significant contribution. Let us warmly welcome them into our political system, support or reject their ideas based on merit, and never ask them to check their faith at the door.

Chapter 6

TELLING RELIGION TO "SHUT UP"

Scott Kline

Scott Kline is the author of *The Ethical Being: A Catholic Guide to Contemporary Issues* (Novalis, 2013). He is associate professor of religious studies and interim Vice President Academic and Dean at St. Jerome's University in the University of Waterloo.

On October 17, 1996, Canadians tuned into their nightly newscast to hear Canadian Broadcasting Corporation (CBC) news anchor Peter Mansbridge say, "Good evening. A blistering attack on governments across the country today, from Canada's Roman Catholic bishops. The issue is poverty. The bishops accuse governments of using the most vulnerable people in society as human fodder in the battle against deficits. And the bishops weren't the only ones speaking out." The Canadian Conference of Catholic Bishops (CCCB) was using the fourth annual United Nations International Day for the Eradication of Poverty as the occasion to release its pastoral letter "The Struggle against Poverty: A Sign of Hope for Our World."[1] The CBC report continued:

> In Canada, more than five million people are poor. More than a million of them are children. The Canadian Conference of Catholic Bishops issued a sharp attack against government policies it says hurt Canada's poor, especially the children ... The bishops quote a report from Church groups, which says, "In our society, if a parent denies a child food, clothing and social security, it is considered child abuse; but when our government denies 1,362,000 children the same, it is simply balancing the budget."

As Joe Gunn, former director of Social Affairs at the CCCB, has recalled, "That statement caused a bit of a stir."[2]

The Canadian bishops' 1996 pastoral letter contained echoes of an earlier seven-page paper called "Ethical Reflections on the Economic Crisis," released on New Year's Day, 1983. The bishops claimed that the government of Prime Minister Pierre Elliott Trudeau had put business interests above the interests of those suffering from poverty and unemployment, which was 12.8 percent at the time. The bishops' paper criticized the Trudeau government's pro-business strategy for putting a "renewed emphasis on the 'survival of the fittest' as the supreme law of economics." The bishops argued that priorities had to be controlling profits, increasing taxes on the rich, allowing for a larger role for labour unions, and establishing a government-backed jobs creation program: "The goal of serving the human needs of all people in our society must take precedence over the maximization of profits and growth." The bishops' criticism of the Canadian government was a front-page story in most daily newspapers in Canada, and was covered in *The New York Times*, *The Washington Post*, *Los Angeles Times*, *Newsweek* and *Time*. Eventually, the CCCB sold 200,000 copies of "Ethical Reflections on the Economic Crisis" and had it translated into seven languages. In spite of the enthusiasm and interest generated by the paper, Prime Minister Trudeau flippantly dismissed the bishops with the terse statement "I don't think their economics are very good." It was, he believed, all he needed to say to make his case to Canadians that religion and ethics are private matters and, for that reason, Catholic bishops have no business meddling in Canada's political and economic affairs.

Shutting religion up isn't easily done. In many respects, it is easier for governments to shut up religious institutions than religious individuals since, in many modern democratic states, religious institutions hold tax-exempt status – and even threatening the removal of that status can effectively muzzle religious authorities. Still, religious people continue to speak out on a wide range of issues that have political and economic consequences: war, peacemaking, poverty, health care, immigration, marriage, labour, trade policy, international development, foreign policy, and the environment. Depending on the issue, politicians can turn themselves inside out trying to manage their relationship with religious actors.

Take reactions to Pope Francis's May 2015 encyclical, *Laudato si'*, for example. Asked by the conservative talk-show host Sean Hannity about Pope Francis's encyclical on climate change, the Republican U.S. presidential candidate Jeb Bush, a Catholic, responded, "I don't get economic policy from my bishops or my cardinal or my pope – I think religion ought to be about making us better as people, less about things [that] end up getting into the political realm."[3] The irony here is that the Republican Party and the Bush family have long appealed to religion, and specifically the Catholic Church, to push a political agenda focused on, among other things, school prayer, family values, abortion, and even U.S. support for Israel.

My concern is that, for the past 20 years, many of the public debates over the relationship between religion and politics in the United States and, increasingly so, in Canada have been filtered through the distorted rhetoric of the "culture wars."[4] In other words, telling religion to "shut up" has become less about society trying to balance democratic freedom and religious authority and more about using religion as a weapon in often petty culture war skirmishes. My aim in this chapter is to shift our thinking away from the culture war narrative and back to a richer discussion that recalls a tradition of us wrestling with the secularization of society.

The Extremism of the Culture Wars

At the 1992 Republican National Convention, which nominated President George H.W. Bush to run for a second term,

Patrick Buchanan set off what is likely the first shot in the current U.S. culture war. Buchanan, a former aide in the Nixon White House turned bombastic political pundit and failed presidential candidate, declared:

> My friends, this election is about much more than who gets what. It is about who we are. It is about what we believe. It is about what we stand for as Americans. There is a religious war going on in our country for the soul of America. It is a cultural war, as critical to the kind of nation we will one day be as was the Cold War itself. And in that struggle for the soul of America, Clinton & Clinton are on the other side, and George Bush is on our side. And so, we have to come home, and stand beside him.

Throughout the 1990s, the political conservatives often rallied around culture war themes – school prayer, gay men and women in the military, abortion, the structure of the family, and federal funding of the arts – to battle the Clinton administration. These culture war battles were, however, generally won by Democrats and Clinton supporters. But under the shrewd political direction of Karl Rove, George W. Bush successfully drew culture war battle lines to create "wedge issues" to win the 2000 and, especially, the 2004 presidential election races.

With the presidential election victories of Barack Obama in 2008 and 2012, conservative culture warriors focused primarily on criticizing the Obama administration's relationship with the Benjamin Netanyahu government in Israel, carving out religious exceptions in the *Affordable Care Act* (the health-care plan commonly known as "Obamacare"), if not actually overturning the Act, and protecting the legal definition of marriage as a heterosexual union. While there have been small wins for conservatives, a series of Supreme Court decisions in June 2015 and a tide of public opinion, especially among younger voters, indicate that "the other side," to use Buchanan's terminology, is nearing complete victory.[5] David Brooks, a *New York Times* columnist with affinities for social and political conservatism, has even begun to outline a strategy for "the next culture war," which focuses less on maintaining a political voice on divisive issues, especially those related to sexuality, and more on helping "reweave the sinews of society." According to Brooks, this culture war would be more "Albert Schweitzer and Dorothy Day than Jerry Falwell and Franklin Graham; more Salvation Army than Moral Majority."[6]

The media have played an integral role in fuelling the current culture wars. For instance, Fox News commentator Bill O'Reilly authored a book in 2006 entitled *Culture Warrior* in which he broke down almost 250 years of debate about the relationship between religion and politics into two factions: traditionalists and secular-progressives. According to O'Reilly, traditionalists believe that the United States is, on the whole, a noble country, that the nuclear family needs protection, and that Christian values can and should inform political, legal, and social decisions. In stark contrast, secular-progressives are socialists, hostile to Christianity, dismissive of traditional American values, and undermining the vision of the country's Founding Fathers. In O'Reilly's opinion, the secular-progressives have seized control of Hollywood, American universities, the media, and, since 2008, the White House, and they are conspiring to silence traditionalists, particularly those with traditional Christian-American values. A recurring example is the so-called war on Christmas. Every

Christmas season, O'Reilly takes the opportunity to run stories of municipalities that have removed Christmas trees from their public spaces and popular retailers that have chosen "Happy Holidays" over "Merry Christmas." This shaming campaign rings true with many Christian conservatives who are fed up with being told to "shut up" in public.

In Canada, the culture war has not been nearly as explosive or widespread as it is in the United States. Nevertheless, skirmishes do occasionally appear over abortion, the CBC, the niqab, the environment, race, gun ownership, religious freedom, and Canada's relationship with Israel. In the lead-up to the 2015 election, these became potential wedge issues in certain parts of the country, especially in ridings with recent immigrant populations who have brought their traditional religious beliefs with them. According to journalist Marci McDonald, culture war battles are only bound to increase in Canada if Conservatives and the Stephen Harper government continue to sidle up to seasoned American culture war activists. In her 2010 book *The Armageddon Factor*, McDonald warns that Prime Minister Stephen Harper has allowed politically conservative evangelicals, a group she calls "Christian nationalists," to play an unprecedented role in shaping Canadian policy. She is convinced that this group, driven by a theocratic vision of government and a political timeline ending in the apocalypse, is attempting to create a Christian nation where "non-believers – atheists, non-Christians, and even Christian secularists – have no place, and those in violation of biblical law, notably homosexuals and adulterers, would merit severe punishment and the sort of shunning that once characterized a society where suspected witches were burned."[7] In essence, her book is an attempt to expose this small, yet influential group of Christian zealots so that true Canadians will silence them. But as Molly Worthen, a historian of North American evangelicalism, has concluded in a review of *The Armageddon Factor* for *The Globe and Mail*, "McDonald sees Christian nationalist conspiracy everywhere she looks."[8] Indeed, McDonald relies heavily on books written by journalists who have oversimplified and distorted evangelical responses to political involvement.

Regrettably, the extremism of the culture wars doesn't allow for nuance. Fuelled by political interests to mobilize a party base behind wedge issues and by various media personalities to garner ratings and readership, the rhetoric of the culture war breeds suspicion, animosity, and intractability. Too often, it simplistically pits "traditionalists" against "secularists," each trying to vanquish the other. Caught up in the culture war rhetoric, it is easy for religious people to conclude that "secularists" are always telling them to shut up. Likewise, it is easy for "secularists" to believe that religious people are always trying to impose some type of theocratic rule on them. The reality, however, is that these are extreme positions. In modern democratic societies, different types of secularism and ways of faith-based political engagement have developed over the past two and a half centuries. Today, we do live in increasingly post-Christian and multicultural societies; yet, for many, religion provides the moral foundations for political action. The remainder of this chapter will help us understand our types of secularism and, in the process, begin to discover productive ways to interact with one another in the public sphere.

Democratic Freedom, Religious Authority, and Secularism

In modern democracies, there exists an often palpable tension between democratic freedom and religious authority. One of the earliest political thinkers to encounter a modern democracy attempting to resolve this tension was the 19th-century French author Alexis de Tocqueville (1805–1859). In 1831, Tocqueville travelled to the United States on a mission to examine prisons on behalf of the French government. His study of prisons, however, soon became secondary to his broader interest in America's rapidly changing social, political, and economic conditions. The result of his extensive travel, which included visits to Upper and Lower Canada, was his classic work *Democracy in America*, first published in 1835.

The political culture Tocqueville encountered in America during the early 1830s was strange. As a French intellectual, he would have assumed that democratic freedom and religious authority were mutually exclusive commitments. To his way of thinking, the French Enlightenment was, if anything, a historical turning point in which human reason was liberated from clerical masters and the institutional dominance of the Catholic Church. But in the United States, Tocqueville saw that the origins of American democracy were fundamentally related to an "infinite variety of ceaselessly changing Christian sects," including the extremist Puritans, which cultivated political difference while maintaining a fervently Christian society. In recognition of this tension between democratic liberty and religious authority, Tocqueville concluded that the structure of religious life of the United States was entirely distinct from the political life, and yet strangely interdependent. The tension that he highlighted in the 1830s stemmed from an older Protestant Reformation debate concerning how Christianity could be reconciled with civil government. While variations exist within the Protestant tradition, one important product of this historical debate was the blending of commitments to popular self-government and religious freedom. As

Hugh Heclo notes in his 2007 book *Christianity and American Democracy*, the United States was the first to organize itself by embracing the "twin tolerations" of democratic freedom and religious autonomy. In effect, America's early twinning of democratic freedom and religious autonomy was, to a large degree, a rejection of a European theocratic political principle: "Because our religion is true, it must united with the power of the state." By contrast, the American Christian said in response, "Because our religion is true, it must do no such thing."[9]

Tocqueville's observations of early 19th-century American political culture, in contrast to French political culture, point to a fact that would become clear only in the 20th century: that is, the process of secularization in modern democracies has taken different paths, thus resulting in various types of secularism.[10] Let me highlight two predominant types: laicism and Judeo-Christian secularism.

Laicism

The type of secularism that Tocqueville had known in France is called *laïcité*. Contemporary laicists trace their view of religion in politics to 18th-century France and the movement of radical democrats to wrest political power away from the Catholic Church. They attempt to create a neutral public space in which religious belief, practices, and institutions have no political standing or significance. In their view, religion belongs solely in the private sphere. Consequently, they regard the mixing of religion and politics as irrational and dangerous. For modern democracies to be effective, religion must be separated from politics and the public sphere must be essentially secular.

Laicism is the type of secularism that strongly influenced Pierre Elliott Trudeau, who in spite of his personal religious devotion was nevertheless opposed, and even at times openly hostile, to the involvement of religion in politics. David Seljak, a Canadian sociologist of religion, argues that Trudeau's understanding of the relationship between religion and politics stems from his experiences of the close collaboration of the Roman Catholic Church and the Quebec state under the leadership of Premier Maurice Duplessis and the heady years leading up to the Quiet Revolution in the 1960s.[11] Like many French Canadians in middle of the 20th century, Trudeau was an advocate of a modern Quebec, which meant increased urbanization, industrialization, and economic commercialization. To Trudeau's way of thinking, Quebec's development had been stifled by a type of tribal, feudalistic social structure that allowed the churches to maintain control over social institutions, including education, health care, and social services. He believed that to achieve a modern Quebec, clericalism and other forms of religious authority had to be removed from politics and other public arenas to allow the drivers of modernization to take effect. In other words, religion had to be relegated to the private sphere, along with the family, nationalism, ethnic identity, and morality, thus leaving politics and business to drive development in the public sphere. Recalling Trudeau's breezy dismissal of the Catholic bishops for dabbling in economic affairs in 1983, this was his way of relegating religious voices to the private sphere.

Judeo-Christian Secularism

Another type of secularism stems from what some scholars call a Judeo-Christian secular tradition. Elizabeth Shakman Hurd, in her 2008 book *The Politics of Secularism in International Relations*, notes that this Judeo-Christian secularism does not attempt to expel religion from public life, although it can be suspicious of religions other than Judaism and Christianity. It does not present the religious-secular divide as a clean, essentialized, and bifurcated relationship, as does laicism. Although this form of secularism can seem counterintuitive, we can see already see glimpses of it in Tocqueville's description of the church–state relationship in 1830s America. That is, Judeo-Christian secularism does not need to invoke Christianity in political debates because it has already determined that it is better for both religion and the state to remain separate. Heclo muses, "Christianity has probably been better for American democracy than American democracy has been for Christianity."[12] In this tradition, as William E. Connolly put it, "the separation of church and state functions to soften sectarian divisions between Christian sects while retaining the civilizational hegemony of Christianity in a larger sense."[13] In other words, even though parts of Western society and culture are no longer under the control of religion, political order in the West remains grounded in a common set of core values with their roots in the Christian tradition.

A classic example of this type of Judeo-Christian secularism is the speech that then-Democratic presidential nominee John F. Kennedy gave on the evening of September 12, 1960, to the Greater Houston Ministerial Association. Kennedy's goal in this speech was to allay the fears of many Protestant Christians who believed that a Catholic president would be beholden to the Vatican and that he would attempt to impose Catholic doctrine on public policy. With a presidential election hanging in the balance, Senator Kennedy opened his speech by identifying what he considered to be the real issues of the campaign: the spread of Communism, the loss of respect for the presidency, hunger, poverty, inadequate housing, education, and space exploration. He said,

> These are the real issues which should decide this campaign. And they are not religious issues – for war and hunger and ignorance and despair know no religious barriers. But because I am a Catholic, and no Catholic has ever been elected president, the real issues in this campaign have been obscured – perhaps deliberately, in some quarters less responsible than this. So it is apparently necessary for me to state once again not what kind of church I believe in – for that should be important only to me – but what kind of America I believe in.

Referencing the 1948 pastoral letter from the U.S. Catholic Bishops entitled *The Christian in Action*,[14] Kennedy stated three beliefs. First, he said he believed in

> an America where the separation of church and state is absolute – where no Catholic prelate would tell the President (should he be Catholic) how to act, and no Protestant minister would tell his parishioners for whom to vote – where no church or church school is granted any public funds or political preference – and where no man is denied public office merely because his religion differs from the President who might appoint him or the people who might elect him.

Second, he believed in a secular state; that is, a state with no official religion and

> where no public official either requests or accepts instructions on public policy from the Pope, the

National Council of Churches or any other ecclesiastical source – where no religious body seeks to impose its will directly or indirectly upon the general populace or the public acts of its officials – and where religious liberty is so indivisible that an act against one church is treated as an act against all.

And third, Kennedy professed a belief in an America that practised religious tolerance, which didn't discriminate between Catholics and anti-Catholics, and didn't splinter off into religiously identified voting blocs. He continued,

> Whatever issue may come before me as president – on birth control, divorce, censorship, gambling, or any other subject – I will make my decision in accordance with these views, in accordance with what my conscience tells me to be the national interest, and without regard to outside religious pressures or dictates. And no power or threat of punishment could cause me to decide otherwise.[15]

My point is this: secularism is not a single, static thing that silences religion. Rather, secularism is a fluid concept that has emerged in different forms as part of the ongoing process of working out the relationship between democratic freedom and religious authority. While some laicists may, in practice, be hostile to religion in the public sphere, for the most part *laïcité* is, in principle, an attempt to create a neutral public sphere where rational-critical debates over matters of the public good take place. For Judeo-Christian secularists, the secular public sphere is intended to protect religion from being silenced by other religions, which is why they discourage any single religion or religious doctrine from gaining control over political institutions and policy.

Conclusion: "Talking the Talk"

So if we are faced with a public sphere that is, at worst, hostile to religion or, at best, suspicious of religion becoming overly influential, how ought religious people talk in the public sphere? At this point I am about to give a short, very much incomplete, and likely unsatisfactory answer: for religious people, the primary challenge is translation. In Western democracies, civil society has become the predominant space for open political debate, and religious persons are among many civil society actors vying for airtime in the democratic cacophony. To attract attention in the secular public sphere, religious actors must be able to translate their moral and political values into a common language – the language of public reason – and make their case before an increasingly diverse and less religious public. To be clear, this burden of translation is not solely the religious actor's. As the sociologist Jürgen Habermas argues, non-religious actors must realize the limits of secular reason and be open to the "truth content" of vibrant world religions.[16] As a matter of public reason, then, telling religion to "shut up" limits potentially new and constructive ways of looking at matters of public concern: freedom, security, prosperity, peace, and well-being. Likewise, as a matter of public reason, religious actors must not assume that references to long-held doctrines, Scripture, or any religious authority will appeal to civil society. In sum, religion has a place in the public sphere, as long as religious actors are able to appeal to public reason and all actors are equipped with an adequate level of religious literacy to understand one another when communication starts to break down.[17]

Chapter 7

PUBLIC ETHICS AS A CANADIAN "PUBLIC THEOLOGY"

David Pfrimmer

David Pfrimmer is professor of public ethics at Waterloo Lutheran Seminary at Wilfrid Laurier University. He has served as a parish pastor, the executive secretary of Lutheran Church in America-Canada Section, director of the Lutheran Office for Public Policy, and most recently as the principal-dean at the Waterloo Lutheran Seminary. He has been involved in advocacy with provincial and federal governments as well as the United Nations for over 25 years, working with the Canadian Council of Churches, the Lutheran World Federation, Kairos, and many multi-faith and NGO coalitions. This chapter is also being published in *Consensus – A Canadian Journal of Public Theology*, November 2015.

Moments for Public Ethics

In June 2012, Canada's Auditor General released a study outlining problems with the expense claims being made by some Senators. These revelations grew into a full-blown scandal when the RCMP charged Senators Mike Duffy, Pamela Wallin, Mac Harb, and Patrick Brazeau with various counts of fraud and breach of trust. A new report by the Auditor General may reveal another five to ten Senators with a "… troublesome pattern of expense claims."[1]

Canada was rocked by the news in October 2014 that Jian Ghomeshi, host of the Canadian Broadcasting Corporation's popular program Q, heard in both Canada and the United States, was fired due to damaging information about his "… predilection for assaulting women and choking women under the guise of sexual encounters."[2] Ghomeshi now faces five criminal charges. In November 2014, federal Liberal leader Justin Trudeau suspended two of his party's MPs over sexual harassment allegations involving two members of the New Democratic Party.

In the wake of incidents at Ferguson, Missouri, and numerous similar tragedies across the United States in which African-Americans have died at the hands of police, the Starbucks coffee chain launched a national "Race Matters" social media campaign to discuss that country's racial divide. While a few applauded this initiative, negative reaction was swift and harsh. Professor Tamara Buckley of the City University of New York noted the importance of creating a meaningful context for such discussions so as to avoid trivializing the issues.[3]

Other sensationalized stories emerging in the media have raised and stimulated very public conversations about the behaviour of leaders, sexual harassment and violence against women, racial tensions, and other significant social questions. There has been no shortage of issues.

What is important to observe and consider here, however, is that unique moments occur when particular questions initiate such crucial conversations that they can change people and the communities in which they live. Conversations like these draw volatile interest and considerable energy from specific segments of society. Especially notable is how quickly and pervasively they come to occupy primary public attention. Public ethics is, in reality, a deeper version of the old water-cooler discussion. Knowing that "everybody is talking about it" is probably among the best indicators that this type of incident creates *a public ethical moment* across all sectors of society. Public ethics is about recognizing and naming such ethical moments and the issues or questions that they present.

A more troubling trait of public ethical moments is that they tend to inspire a rush to judgment. Many commentators appear quite comfortable in pronouncing conclusions without a clear articulation or grasp of the issue(s) at hand, to say nothing of disrespecting "due process." In some cases, it seems as if those in charge were even "making up the process as they went along." Positions were asserted without full knowledge of the allegations, the parties involved, the background circumstances, or other significant details. Over time, some facts were revealed with greater clarity and logic, but the troubling outcome was that the public had largely made up its mind by then ... even if its mind had been proven wrong.

Admittedly, such matters – particularly those involving sexual conduct – can be awkward at best and incendiary at worst. Broadly speaking, the task of public ethics is to help "name the question": that is, assist leaders in animating public discussion(s), enable collective participation in responsible deliberations, and identify appropriate resolutions or outcomes. So public ethics is not just about government, public policy, or public institutions. It needs also to provide form, function, and public purpose to the wider conversations it invokes.

In this paper I will argue that public ethics creates "publics" that encourage a community-based process of moral engagement and deliberation in order to address compelling personal and/or social ethical dilemmas and paradoxes. Such moments draw on our deepest convictions and values in the effort to resolve issues of misery and meaning in our world. Doing public ethics has important implications for faith communities as they find themselves "disestablished" in a very different social context and seeking to identify contributions they can make to enhance the lives of all who live in pluralistic societies like Canada.

I have identified four points to introduce the concept of public ethics:

1. Public ethics is **public.** Its task is to create publics that encourage community-based moral engagement and deliberation in order to address compelling personal and social ethical dilemmas or paradoxes.
2. Public ethics is **ethics**. It enlists our ultimate convictions and deepest values as global citizens in addressing issues and/or resolving life questions about misery and meaning in our world.

3. Public ethics is **theological**. For many Canadians, particularly those who identify as spiritual but not religious, public ethics offers a means to construct ultimate meaning in their lives. It is a way of popularizing or doing theology in a common key, where theology is understood as "faith seeking understanding."[4]
4. Public ethics is about **enhancing** the flourishing of life and our sense of belonging as global citizens.

Public Ethics is *Public*

We generally associate the term "public" with government or government-supported institutions. Universities, schools, hospitals, and civic, provincial/territorial, and federal agencies are considered public – as in public schools or public hospitals. Activities associated with these institutions or other civic processes are considered public – as in public service.

I have chosen, however, to use "public" in a different way, one that returns to its origins. Philosopher Charles Taylor, for example, describes the public sphere as having "extra-political status" – beyond the political, but necessary to its effective functioning.[6] Thus a "public" is much more than its governments, institutions, or civics. Various publics serve as the circulatory system of the body politic, its society, and its culture.

Recently, there has been renewed interest in the nature of our public(s). The term "public sphere" owes much to the 18th-century Enlightenment. Taylor describes it as "… a common space in which members of society are deemed to meet through a variety of media: print, electronic and also face-to-face encounters; to discuss matters of common interest; and thus to be able to form a common mind about these."[6]

He argues that the emergence of public opinion during the 1700s was crucial to creating a common public space that transcends the limitation of "topical spaces." This meta-topical common space is where people, unrelated by family or tribe, can come together "... in a common act of focus for whatever purpose."[7] Taylor's broad and dynamic definition of "public" as a voluntary association of individuals gathered around an idea, purpose, or action is ideally suited to the parameters of my discussion, for in the process of gathering, the members of this public are changed, while at the same time changing their context.

A public can take many forms. Sports leagues, voluntary organizations, service clubs, and faith communities are all, in essence, publics. There can also be publics within publics, such as those existing within organizations that have local, regional, national, and international expressions. But publics are not always positive or constructive; some support negative concepts such as racism, social exclusion, elitism, economic inequality, violence, and exploitation. These associations reflect a darker reality of human publics.

Creating publics and an enabling environment for participation in them is essential for any society. Increasingly, however, we can no longer presume that the publics within any society will exist in a monolithic or permanent nature. For example, Canadian political parties have changed the perception of who their publics are. They no longer presume to broadcast their message to one generic audience, or recruit one-commitment-fits-all volunteers, or even assume to retain the loyalty of those whose families have always supported them, no matter what.

While political parties today understand the need to nurture various publics, not all their party responses are constructive in terms of building a healthy "body politic." Political commentator Susan Delacourt cautions that some current political marketing practices veer "... dangerously close to the view of consumers as morons ... It divides the country into 'niche' markets and abandons the hard political work of knitting together broad consensus or national vision."[8] Such approaches may not serve the best interests of the publics being created.

Today's leaders and organizations need to better understand the dynamic, ongoing, and increasingly complex social process of "making publics."[9] Creating, identifying, and sustaining vibrant publics have become essential skills for leaders in various sectors. In fact, the art and science of "making publics" will present an urgent challenge in the near future to virtually every human institution we know – including those built on the precepts of faith.

Public ethics can thus play a pivotal role in the creation and sustaining of publics that proactively engage, challenge, and collaborate with one another, thereby creating communities. This is often what is meant by references to the "business community," "university community," "LGBTQ community," or other groups that the media and society identify as being gathered around a shared interest or concern.

At some point, leaders also need to be attentive to the life cycle of their publics. Just as publics emerge, they also can and do come to an end. Nowhere is this more evident today than in the changing nature of Canadian rural communities. Many former publics in these communities (church, school, farm organizations, etc.) are dramatically changing or disappearing. Accompanying publics at the end of their lives is as important as attending to end-of-life processes for individual people.

The nature of this public-on-public engagement may at times soar to heights of great inspiration or descend to levels of profound disappointment. It is not always a harmonious cycle, nor is it without controversy or serious differences. Diversities and differences that enlist our deepest passions and most profound commitments are what make public issues compelling and controversial. Collaborations by publics can also be inspiring, such as the widespread global responses to catastrophic earthquakes in Haiti and Nepal, to name just two recent examples. These are public traits that make participatory societies and democratic politics possible.

Likewise, a concept of public ethics that leads to engagement also facilitates the personal and social changes so essential to community survival; this is what is meant by "politics" in a broader sense than merely the electoral process that forms governments. Public ethics summons our various publics into a level of political engagement that can lead to moral deliberation and action. People are changed, as are the places where they live. *Public* ethics is about these human and non-human relationships.

Public Ethics is *Ethics*

Ethics is often described as the process of discerning how one should live "the good life," about choosing "good" and avoiding "evil," or knowing "right" from "wrong." We have all heard it said of someone that at a critical moment, they "did the right thing!" But the real question is: How do you know what "the right thing" is? Public ethics is not based simply on intuition, although it does require the application of intuition at such challenging moments. Public ethics provides a moral framework for the work of reflection, deliberation, and the *doing* of ethics in a wide variety of ways.

In general, ethics takes place at points where our ultimate convictions and most deeply held values encounter the world's most difficult and profound issues. Christians, for example, take their direction from the Bible and the life and ministry of Jesus; Muslims consult the Holy Qur'an and *hadith* (recorded sayings) of the Prophet Muhammad; Jews turn to the Torah and a long tradition of rabbinical writings.

People are fundamentally social in nature and individuals engage with one another as active participants in a community; in doing so, we transcend the moment of encounter and appropriate a broader worldview and sense of ourselves. Encounters with others and with our own context express and inform who we are (identity), what we do (purpose), and our ultimate goals (hope).

In day-to-day life, our "customary morality," as expressed in laws, regulations, traditions, and culture, is sufficient to express and inform how we conduct ourselves, the choices we make, and what we consider to be important.[10] However, there are other unique moments when our customary morality no longer addresses urgent life questions, such as the existence of misery that challenges our understanding of love, power, and justice. Why is there such suffering? How can such evil exist? How do we address injustice? There are also life questions of meaning that focus on identity, purpose, and destination. Who am I? What is my purpose? What matters in life?

These profound existential questions arise in "ethical" or "theological" moments when we are forced to reconsider our foundational assumptions and worldview. "Life questions are the questions Google can't answer!"[11] They are religious in that they deal with ultimate commitments, convictions, and values. In such moments, life questions are what give vitality to our faith and spirituality. I have often told my students that the most important theological question is "How have I changed my mind and why have I changed it?" These theological or ethical moments are when such self-interrogations can occur. Public ethics takes these moments seriously, as they set the stage for our collective public pursuits.

As with ethics in general, the first task in the interrogative process of public ethics is to describe, and hopefully understand, what is really happening. The great temptation around current Canadian and U.S. scandals – such as those involving disgraced CBC host Jian Ghomeshi, some members of the Senate, or the Starbucks coffee chain – is the great temptation to rush to conclusions or take premature action. Public ethics presses us to get the facts, to probe the context, to be more analytical and deliberative. Buffalo Springfield's famous 1967 protest song "For What It's Worth" captures the problem in its iconic opening lines: "There's something happening here / But what it is ain't exactly clear."

The critical task of ethics in general, and public ethics in particular, lies in identifying the central question revealed in the ambiguity or paradox of the named moment. Clarifying the issue or question that demands to be addressed is crucial to the effectiveness of the ethical enterprise. This is not a solitary process carried out by individuals, but one that necessitates dialogue with others and with other publics. Such "communities of moral deliberation" are essential to public ethics. Lutheran ethicist Ron Duty has written extensively about how churches and congregations need to be communities of moral deliberation.[12] During the civil rights movement, barbershops in African-American communities often served such a role for men, while the local launderette frequently served women as a safe venue for moral discussion.

In identifying and addressing the question, public ethics is not merely public opinion. It enlists 1) experience, 2) reason and cross-disciplinary inquiry, 3) tradition/culture, and 4) sacred texts – our own and those of others. In today's globalized society, public ethics is increasingly both contextual and *trans*contextual.

Public ethics embraces the full range of ethical methodologies, each of which helps to clarify different aspects of the ethical question(s) at hand. Deontology emphasizes respect for rules, while teleological ethics fosters serious consideration of the consequences in hopes of motivating "good" actions. Virtue or character ethics suggests that "when you can't be sure, be responsible!"[13] Much as an automotive transmission applies different gears for different road conditions, these various ethical approaches all contribute to the task of public ethics. Public ethics offers a framework in which to consider how various ethical methodologies can be effectively utilized in the wider arena of discerning "the good life."

Public ethics enlists both personal and social ethics. Most of us can identify with personal ethics in those moments when we apply customary morality and seemingly make autonomous choices. However, human beings are also relational creatures, living in larger communities with many social, economic, political, and environmental systems. In these circumstances, a personal moral code can be insufficient to explain or even be effective in the actual doing of ethics.

There are structural and systemic questions that impact life's flourishing. During the 1960s, University of Chicago ethicist Gibson Winter began to speak more about the importance of a "social ethics" that "… deals with issues of social order – good, right, ought in the organization of human communities and the shaping of social policies. Hence the subject matter of social ethics is moral rightness and goodness in shaping human society."[14] Since personal and social ethics are very interdependent in our world, I suggest that public ethics incorporates both their questions and issues. Yet in other ways, public ethics transcends both as well, offering a more dynamic, interactive, and wider collective process of deliberation and action. In a sense, public ethics provides a framework that moves us towards wider theological considerations.

Public Ethics is *Public Theology*

Public ethics is *public*. Public ethics is *ethics*. I can argue further that for many Canadians, particularly for those who consider themselves spiritual but not religious, public ethics is also *theological*. St. Anselm of Canterbury (1033–1109) best summarized the task of theology as "faith seeking understanding" (*fides quaerens intellectum*).[15] Public ethics is spiritual or religious as it involves the ultimate values and convictions of publics that exist within and across faith traditions. Many people today have limited engagement with their religious institutions and communities, or are even estranged from them. Doing public ethics may be a viable alternative theological architecture for them in making meaning and understanding their world.

In the 1960s, Reinhold Niebuhr made a similar observation in terms of the role ethics might play. "Ethics," Niebuhr argued,

> is troubled by these questions because religion is concerned with life and existence as a unity and coherence of meaning. In so far as it is impossible to live at all without presupposing a meaningful existence, the life of every person is religious, with the possible exception of the rare skeptic who is more devoted to the observation of life than to living it, and whose interest in detailed facts is more engrossing than his concern for ultimate meaning and coherence. Even such persons have usually constructed a little cosmos in a world which they regard as chaos and derive vitality and direction from their faith in the organizing purpose of this cosmos.[16]

Public ethics carries a similar theological potential for making meaning in our current context.

In the midst of huge advances in science, technology, and knowledge, people are searching for greater understanding and, dare I say, wisdom. As sociologist Rodney Stark notes, "There are some questions only the gods can answer!"[17] And many who are asking important theological questions are not looking to traditional sources and institutions. As Canadian sociologist Reginald Bibby has pointed out, "Across the country, some 7 in 10 adults and more than 5 in 10 teens explicitly indicate that they have spiritual needs…."[18]

In fact, "spirituality" is replacing religion as the preferred descriptor of such needs. A 2012 Forum research poll done for the *National Post* "shows two-thirds of Canadians are spiritual while just half say they are religious."[19] Forum President Lorne Bozinoff observes that

> Organized religion is on the decline, but when we talk about spirituality that is a whole different ball game. These people [spiritual but not religious] don't believe in organized religions' view of God. But they still fear death – big questions around things like that – and I think those kinds of things keep people spiritual, even though they might not be religious.[20]

Bibby's assessment is that while there is revived interest in religion and spirituality, people are not looking to traditional institutional providers to meet these needs.

The diminished authority of religious leaders and institutions is not unique to faith communities. Peter C. Newman described a revolution that took place among Canadians between 1985 and 1995:

> During the decade under review, Canadians individually and collectively lost common cause with their institutions. Divorced from their sense of God, King and Country – thus separated from their sense of religion, monarchy and land – Canadians carried their own Cross, wore their own Crown, and held their own orb.[21]

This "revolution" distanced Canadians from their institutions, resulting in their former deference towards authorities being replaced by distrust and defiance of those authorities. Nowhere is this more evident than in Canadians' participation in and attitudes towards historic church organizations. Statistics Canada reports that in the General Social Survey (GSS), "… 21% of Canadians aged 15 and over reported they attended a religious service at least once a week in 2005, down from 30% in 1985."[22] But we also see this trend in other institutions, such as political parties, service clubs, and other voluntary organizations, with the possible exception of team sports leagues. Robert Putnam has described this change in the U.S. as "bowling alone," whereby people are less inclined to belong to organizations – even bowling leagues![23]

Canadians nevertheless remain concerned about their social well-being and the health of the planet. In 2012, the Environics Institute, in partnership with other organizations, conducted a poll asking what it meant "to be a Canadian citizen in Canada." Here is what they found:

> When presented with a list of 17 candidate attributes of a good citizen in Canada, treating men and women equally (95% say this is very important to being a good citizen in Canada) is at the top of the list, followed by obeying Canada's laws (89%), being tolerant or respectful of others who are different (82%), voting in elections (82%) and protecting the environment (80%). Majorities of between six and seven in 10 each say a good citizen pays attention to current issues (68%), respects other religions (65%), feels connected to others in society (63%) and knows about Canada's history (62%).
>
> Half of Canadians each say being a good citizen means actively participating in the local community (51%), sharing common values (51%), displaying pride in Canada (e.g. celebrating Canada Day) (51%) or volunteering (49%), while four in 10 each say it includes giving to charity (42%) and learning about Aboriginal peoples (40%). Being bilingual (English

and French) (19%) and being an entrepreneur or a small business owner (18%) are found at the bottom of the list.[24]

Canadians remain committed to a vision of the "peaceable kingdom." Articulating the structure or meaning, and the networks of relationships to sustain that vision, will be increasingly important.

Bibby has made the important observation that the problem in Canada is not secularization *per se*, but polarization. He writes:

> Canada is experiencing a growing level of religious polarization ... The more significant question that is potentially of interest to just about everyone is the question of consequences – the implications for the quality of personal and collective life, starting with the ability of people who are religious, and those who are not, to co-exist.[25]

Insofar as life questions of human misery and meaning are shared by both the traditionally faithful and the spiritual but not religious, public ethics may provide some common space to bridge this polarized divide. For example, Canadian churches were leaders in the anti-apartheid movement, but this initiative also enlisted labour unions, non-governmental organizations, and other social justice groups. If spiritual needs are important to people, are there less assertive and more engaging alternatives by which to address them? I suggest that "public ethics" might serve as the gateway to a Canadian public theology of meaning-making, without foreclosing access to the existing resources held by faith traditions.

Public Ethics in the *Public Commons*

What should be evident at this point is that faith remains a very public matter with a distinct role to play, even if its institutional expressions in Canada seem to be waning in influence and vitality and the historic providers are changing. But how will communities of faith respond to or identify their roles in this context? This is a much larger conversation. However, I argue that there is a new public architecture, which I have called the "public commons." (See Figure 1.)[26]

![Figure 1: The Public Commons diagram showing Economic Actors (Competition), Civil Society Actors (Cooperation), Faith Group Actors (Meaning), and Government Actors (Order) surrounding a central Public Commons containing Markets, Civic Engagement, Voluntary Service, and Religious Life. Callouts identify "Church/State Relationship" and "Public Ethics as a Canadian Public Theology." The Public Commons is that open space where publics emerge to articulate the collective narrative(s), envision the common good and engage the public purpose albeit to do "public ethics."]

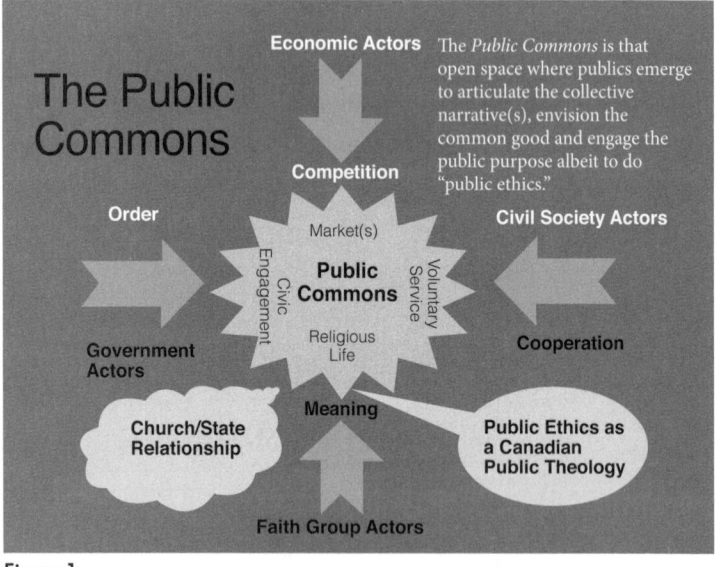

Figure 1

The *public commons* is that open space where publics emerge to articulate their collective narrative(s), envision the common good and engage the public purpose; that is, to do "public ethics." Government, economic, social, and faith-based actors engage each other in addressing the broader political, economic, societal, and ethical issues this entails. The commons is illustrative, not definitive, in that individual and community actors occupy multiple social locations in the various sectors that attend the public commons.

What is important is that within this framework, the participation of faith groups in the public commons is informed by a public theology, or theologies. For Christian communities, this conversation begins with this question: What does it mean to be a "public church" with an appropriate "public theology"?[27] Globalization has resulted in many currents and dynamics that are causing significant changes in our local, regional, and national contexts. Faith communities bring both strength and vulnerability into this new reality, one in which they will inevitably play a public role.

Having a public theology will be important in shaping and informing that new public role. But what exactly do we mean by a "public theology"? A burgeoning field of study has arisen around this question, giving rise to diverse perspectives that are often conditioned by particular circumstances and contexts. Theologian Jürgen Moltmann offers one definition that may serve our purposes:

> A *theologia publica*, a public theology ... gets involved in the public affairs of society. It thinks about what is of general concern in the light of hope in Christ for the Kingdom of God. It becomes political in the name of the poor and marginalized in a given society. Remembrance of the Crucified Christ makes it critical toward political religions and idolatries. It thinks critically about the religious and moral values of societies in which it exists, and presents its reflections as a reasoned position.[28]

It will be our emerging public theology that informs and shapes the participation of faith communities in the public commons. Historically, churches and faith communities have embraced a "political theology" to serve as an imperative for their civic role and contribution. But given the disestablishment of religious institutions, along with broader changes in social and cultural dynamics, another question arises: Is there an emerging distinct Canadian public theology to inform and guide faith communities in their future contributions to the public commons?

I propose that public ethics might serve to guide and shape just such a Canadian *theologia publica*. Undertaken with humility and deference, a distinctly Canadian public theology would create, nurture, sustain, animate, and accompany its constituent publics in the process of modelling how public ethics should be done. This could be a significant positive contribution by faith communities to the important work of the public commons. Likewise, it may result in a renewed means for overcoming polarization, becoming the new theological *lingua franca* for those seeking to make meaning in an emerging and quite different Canadian religious landscape.

Public Ethics as a Summons to Global Citizenship

Why is public ethics so important in this age of seemingly private morality? What difference will public ethics make as the *lingua franca* of a renewed public theology? More thought is needed around the concept of public ethics and its implications. At this point, however, at least four preliminary contributions warrant further consideration: 1) public ethics offers authoritative narratives or worldviews around "belonging"; 2) public ethics can offer a new paradigm for community leadership; 3) public ethics can offer a new framework for validating public participation; and 4) public ethics can help foster authenticity, civility, and integrity within political systems.

Let us consider some initial thoughts on each of these contributions.

First, an important theological contribution of public ethics is to enlist people into a *broader authoritative narrative* of their respective public or community. A significant social disease of our time is a profound sense of existential loneliness, or not belonging. Engaging in public ethics as a process of creating, nurturing, and sustaining our publics may give us a better sense of who we are, what we are called to do, and the ultimate goal of our lives. In short, it might provide people with a means of belonging to something larger than themselves in a world that wants to relegate them to being mere entities, consumers, and taxpayers.

The concept of global citizenship captures a fuller notion of this belonging. In her 2014 Massey Lectures series, published as *Belonging: The Paradox of Citizenship*, former broadcast journalist and Canadian governor general Adrienne Clarkson described our fundamental "paradox" this way:

> The greatest challenge for us is to understand and satisfy both our natural competitive instincts and this deep longing for cooperation … Life at its best exists in cooperative, sharing, and balanced relationships with other lives. This interdependence we call belonging.[29]

In its interdependent origins, public ethics differs from theological ethics, in that theological ethics emerges from and is applied according to a particular faith perspective. Public ethics becomes a theological narrative arising from the gathering of a public; it summons people to lives as global citizens, affirming their agency through a commitment to the public purpose and common good.

Second, public ethics offers a new paradigm for what I describe as *community leadership*. Peter C. Newman's 1995 book *The Canadian Revolution: From Deference to Defiance* led to widespread doubts about all those in positions of authority and leadership. People became, and continue to be, unwilling to defer to leaders who think they know what is best for them, their organization, community, or country. Many polls have shown decreased public confidence in leaders across various sectors, including faith communities.[30] Sociologist David Seljak notes a similar skepticism around religious leaders. "Bishops can make whatever pronouncements they want, but even the people in the pews aren't listening ... Even their most loyal followers are deciding for themselves."[31]

In the same vein, public acceptance of the old paternal leadership paradigm is changing to one of "accompaniment," with the key question being: How can leaders accompany publics in their process of convening, deliberating, and acting? What this new leadership modality will look like is admittedly unclear. More certain is the expectation that an accompaniment model of community leadership will be different and may require its own public to articulate it. Community leadership will be important in many settings, particularly for religious leadership and the revitalization of faith communities.

In a presentation I gave several years ago on the future of theological education, I argued that Canadian churches may require pastors to be less like "shepherds" (the paternalist model) and more like "adventure guides" (the community leadership model), helping people explore beyond their comfort zones to experience new places and different ideas and sources of meaning.[32] Another example is that of Ronald Heifetz at the John F. Kennedy School of Government at Harvard, who speaks of "adaptive leadership."[33]

Third, public ethics offers a means of *understanding, authenticating, and validating public participation* in the political process. Many writers have raised questions about the health of Canadian democracy. Again, Susan Delacourt has highlighted the problem of narrowcasting and marketing political messages at targeted consumer-citizens, thereby eliminating wider and more broadly inclusive conversations.[34] Alison Loat and Michael MacMillan conducted exit interviews with former Members of Parliament and noted some of the "failings" of Canadian democracy. They observed that in his time, John A. Macdonald needed his MPs to communicate with constituents. In our age of social media, this role for the MP has largely disappeared.[35] Journalist Chris Hedges sums up the essential problem:

> What endures is not the fact of democratic liberalism but the myth of it. The myth is used by corporate power elites and their apologists to justify the subjugation and manipulation of other nations in the name of national self-interest and democratic values … the assault of the corporate state on the democratic state claimed the liberal class as one of its victims.[36]

Declining voter participation and other indicators further reveal the erosion of our democratic institutions.

Public ethics understands that "liberal democracy" is one form that public participation can take. The important dynamic to bear in mind is the element of public participation. Federal Green Party leader Elizabeth May believes (as do many others) that "Public policy is no longer being developed through a process reflecting the public will. Nor is it being developed based on what the country needs in response to issues of concern ...." May's observation points to a source of the cynicism today and the need for a public ethics that can offer a new politics with potentially greater participation because it understands how people participate, why they participate, and what they can contribute.[37]

Finally, a public ethics that offers an authoritative narrative, community leadership opportunities, and enhanced public participation can provide *a greater sense of belonging for people and communities.* As professor Christopher Ross once told me, "politics is the grammar of human relationships."[38] Thus new kinds of relationships might enable new kinds of politics, characterized by authenticity, integrity, and civility. While belonging is not without its darker side – as Michael Ignatieff noted about the sometimes violent connection between nationalism and belonging[39] – in belonging to dynamic publics, we might rediscover the gift and joy of citizenship and our shared hopes for Canada and the world. In belonging, we might better understand what is at stake for our common future. Chilean economist Manfred Max-Neef points to the difference between knowledge in the midst of separateness and the understanding that comes with belonging: "Never in human history has there been such an accumulation of knowledge like in the last 100 years ... the point is that knowledge alone is not enough, we lack understanding ... When you belong, you understand. When you're separated, you can accumulate knowledge."[40]

Public ethics therefore must contribute to a progressive and constructive sense of belonging, where greater numbers of people connected to a multiplicity of publics can collectively serve the common good.

In conclusion, a process of public ethics that enhances life's flourishing and belonging may be what faith communities can bring to the public commons. Such a public ethics could address crises of misery and meaning by affirming the identity, agency, and visions that make us truly human. Faith communities have a tradition and imperative for reaching out to the stranger, the widow, the orphan, and all who are considered "other."

Reginald Bibby recalls a column by *Toronto Star* writer Carol Goar in which she points out that "faith based organizations are the bedrock of Canada's charitable sector." They provide all kinds of services: from homeless shelters, to sponsoring and resettling refugees, to running facilities for the elderly, providing care for the young, food programs for the poor, and a host of other services. Gore concludes with some strong words: "It is fine to say – as a majority of Canadians do – that you prefer to explore your own spirituality, practice your religion privately and ponder metaphysical questions in solitude." But, she says, "... look around. There is a world in need out there. Church members are on the front lines, putting their faith to work. They could use some help."[41] Offering to accompany people in their life adventures may indeed revitalize the public roles of both religious leaders and their faith communities.

I have argued here that public ethics is *public*, taking seriously how publics are formed and reformed. I have noted that public ethics is *ethics*, in that it offers a new architecture for conceptualizing the field of ethics. Given the growing number of spiritual but not religious people in our midst, public ethics may be an alternative theological means for addressing life questions of misery and meaning. The aim of public ethics is to enhance life's flourishing and the sense of belonging. "Nothing is anything without everything!" as Larry Rasmussen has said. Finally, I have suggested some implications of practising public ethics in terms of an authoritative narrative, a paradigm of community leadership for authenticating and validating new forms of public participation and for developing a new politics.

Such a vision of public ethics does not require its practitioners or advocates to be "religious," or even people of faith. As Bibby points out, "… people can be good without God."[42] Certainly, we could find evidence of public ethics being practised in other places. However, public ethics is also rooted in the tradition of mainline churches in particular and faith communities in general. To say they have some experience in doing ethics is a vast understatement. Developing and bringing a public ethics to the commons may help to foster a more deliberative and less reactive response to some of the more pressing scandals and incendiary issues of our day. This 21st-century world is a wonderfully dangerous, troubling, yet exciting place. The rise of a new public ethics could be the embodiment of Canadian theologian Douglas Hall's hope in a renewed vocation for Canadian churches and religious communities:

> In Canada today a church freed from ethnic, economic, class, and other interests and identities could function as a forum for caring in the midst of a society in crisis … Such a church could be a companion in the night to a society which is afraid of the dark.[43]

Endnotes

Introduction

1. Quoted in Michael Kirwan, *Political Theology: An Introduction* (Minneapolis: Fortress Press, 2009), 34.
2. Pope Francis, Morning Meditation in the Chapel of the Domus Sanctae Marthe, Monday, September 16, 2013. See http://en.radiovaticana.va/storico/2013/09/16/pope_francis_christians_must_pray_for_their_leaders/en1-728870 (accessed August 14, 2015).

Chapter 1

1. Cornelius Jaenen, *The Role of the Church in New France* (Toronto: McGraw-Hill Ryerson, 1976), 16 and 42.
2. John S. Moir, ed., *Church and State in Canada, 1627–1867* (Ottawa: McClelland and Stewart, Carleton Library, No. 33, 1967), 111–58.
3. Moir, *Church and State*, 77.
4. Hilda Neatby, *The Quebec Act: Protest and Policy* (Scarborough: Prentice-Hall, 1972).
5. R.J. Morgan, "Lawrence Kavanagh," *Dictionary of Canadian Biography*, Vol. VI (1821–1835) http://www.biographi.ca/en/bio/kavanagh_laurence_6E.html (accessed August 14, 2015).
6. John S. Moir, "The Canadianization of the Protestant Churches," Canadian Historical Association, *Annual Report* (1966): 56–69.
7. Sharon Anne Cook, *Through Sunshine and Shadow: The Women's Christian Temperance Union, Evangelicalism, and Reform in Ontario, 1874–1930* (Montreal & Kingston: McGill-Queen's University Press, 1995).
8. Paul Laverdure, *Sunday in Canada: The Rise and Fall of the Lord's Day* (Gravelbourg, SK: Gravelbooks, 2004).
9. Egerton Ryerson, *Report on a System of Public Elementary Instruction* (1846) in J.G. Hodgins, *A Documentary History of Education in Upper Canada*, Vol. 6 (Toronto, 1911), 149–50.
10. Franklin Walker, *Catholic Education and Politics in Upper Canada* (Toronto: Catholic Educational Foundation of Ontario, 1955), 310–11.
11. Robert T. Dixon, *We Remember, We Believe: A History of Toronto's Catholic Separate School Boards* (Toronto: TCDSB, 2007), 11.
12. John S. Moir, "Toronto's Protestants and Their Perceptions of Their Catholic Neighbours," in Mark G. McGowan and Brian P. Clarke, eds., *Catholics at the Gathering Place: Historical Essays on the Archdiocese of Toronto, 1841–1991* (Toronto: CCHA, 1993), 323; Ramon Hathorn, "Sarah Bernhardt and the

Bishops of Montreal and Quebec," CCHA *Historical Studies*, 53 (1986): 97–120.

13 Mark G. McGowan, "Air Wars: Radio Regulation, Sectarianism and Religious Broadcasting in Canada, 1922–1938," Canadian Society of Church History, *Papers* (2008): 5–26.

14 *Hansard*, May 31, 1928, 3619–20.

15 Roger Bird, ed., *Documents of Canadian Broadcasting*, "Aird Commission Report" (Ottawa: Carleton University Press, 1988), 50.

16 Library and Archives Canada, RG 41, Vol. 146, file 9–10, Acting Secretary M. Landry to All Broadcasting Stations in Canada, December 23, 1936.

17 Mark G. McGowan, "The Fulton Sheen Affair: Religious Controversy, Nationalism and Commercialism in the Early Years of Canadian Television, 1952–1958," CCHA *Historical Studies* 75 (2009): 21–38.

18 Dorothy Zolf and Paul W. Taylor, "Redressing the Balance in Canadian Broadcasting: A History of Religious Broadcasting Policy in Canada," *Studies in Religion/Sciences Religieuses*, 18, no. 2 (June 1989): 153–70.

19 Richard Allen, *The Social Passion: Religion and Social Reform in Canada, 1914–1928* (Toronto: University of Toronto Press, 1973).

20 Gregory Baum, *Catholics and Canadian Socialism* (Toronto: Lorimer, 1980).

21 Robert J. Ogle, *North/South Calling* (Saskatoon: Fifth House, 1987).

22 Alphonse de Valk, csb, "Understandable but Mistaken: Law, Morality and the Canadian Catholic Church 1966–1969," CCHA, *Study Sessions*, 49 (1982): 87–110.

23 Social Affairs Commission, Canadian Conference of Catholic Bishops, "Ethical Reflections on the Economic Crisis," in E.F. Sheridan, SJ, ed., *Do Justice! The Social Teaching of the Canadian Catholic Bishops* (Sherbrooke, QC: Editions Paulines, 1987), 399–410; Tony Clarke, *Behind the Mitre: The Moral Leadership Crisis in the Canadian Catholic Church* (Toronto: HarperCollins, 1995), 69.

24 James Mulligan, CSC, *Catholic Education: The Future Is Now* (Toronto: Novalis, 1999), 63–76.

25 *Toronto Star*, November 4, 2014.

26 Janet Epp-Buckingham, "How Fundamental Is Freedom of Religion?" Saskatchewan Institute of Public Policy (May 2007).

27 David Seljak, "Why the Quiet Revolution was 'Quiet': The Catholic Church's Reaction to the Secularization of Quebec After 1960," CCHA *Historical Studies*, 62 (1996): 109–24.

28 *Catholic Register*, September 24, 2014.

29 Bill Blaikie, "Ambushing the Messenger," *Convivium*, Vol.1, No.1 (March 2012): 5.

30 Marci McDonald, "Jesus in the House: Is the Religious Right Taking Over Stephen Harper's Government?" *The Walrus*, Vol. 3, No. 8 (October 2006): 44–60.

31 Susan Delacourt, *Shopping for Votes: How Politicians Choose Us and We Choose Them* (Madeira Park, BC: Douglas & McIntyre, 2013), 11 and 277. Delacourt makes no mention of recruiting religious groups in the general trolling for votes, but it is evident in Michael Harris, *Party of One: Stephen Harper and Canada's Radical Makeover* (Toronto: Viking, 2014), 43–44.

32 *Toronto Star*, April 23, 2011.

33 Mark Noll, "What Happened to a Christian Canada?" *Church History*, Vol. 75, No. 2 (June 2006): 273.

Chapter 2

1 Numerous religious accommodations sparked the "Accommodation Crisis": "Wearing the veil at school, the sukkah, the eiruv, the rabbinical schools, the wearing of the kirpan, the Sikh turban instead of a helmet at the Port of Montreal, grants to schools reserved exclusively for students of Jewish obedience …, frosted windows at the YMCA [gym] due to the presence of young Hasidic Jews in the courtyard of the neighbouring synagogue; the written recommendation of the police department of the City of Montreal to its policewomen to appeal to their male colleagues' patrol when Hasidic Jews wanted to talk only to male police officers; the schedule for public swimming in the City of Montreal, modified to reserve certain hours exclusively for female customers in order to accommodate Muslim swimmers; prohibiting the presence of husbands during prenatal classes due to the presence of Muslim women in the local community centre Parc-Extension; providing places for prayer and the use of washrooms to wash feet at l'École de technologie supérieure; the exemption given to some Muslim students, for religious reasons, to play the flute in a music class; the borough of Outremont which, to accommodate Jews going to the synagogue on the Sabbath, decided to superimpose the signs prohibiting auto parking in the vicinity of the synagogue; and finally the examiner of the Company of Quebec Automobile Insurance was obliged to sit in the backseat of the vehicle when conducting a driving test with a Hasidic Jew." This non-exhaustive compilation was made in 2007 by Paul Bégin, « Laïcité et accommodements raisonnables », *Éthique publique. Revue internationale d'éthique sociétale et gouvernementale*, vol. 9, no. 1 (printemps 2007): 158–59. Author's translation.

2 M. Chiasson, "The Management of Diversity in a Pluralist Society: The Quebec Experience, 2007–2014": http://canadianicon.org/table-of-contents/the-management-of-diversity (accessed September 8, 2015).

3 In 2012, Action démocratique du Québec was absorbed by the newly founded (2011) Coalition Avenir Québec.
4 Namely, gender equality, freedom from religion and community pressure, privatized faith and publicized common good.
5 Or at least partly at play. The blame, some argued, had to be shared. If it wasn't for the media's appetite for high ratings and sensationalism, none of the heated debates over State neutrality, common and public culture, rights and duties of the host society and immigrants would have taken place. The media, some say, misled what was already anxious public opinion by manufacturing religious accommodation problems that could have been effectively treated, but were rather instrumentalized politically (M. Potvin and M. Tremblay, *Crise des accommodements raisonnables : une fiction médiatique ?* [Outremont, QC: Éditions Athéna, 2008]; G. Bouchard and C. Taylor, *Fonder l'avenir. Le temps de la conciliation*, Rapport de la Commission de consultation sur les pratiques d'accommodement reliées aux différences culturelles [Québec, 2008].
6 CROP–*La Presse* survey, February 14, 2014.
7 J. Baubérot and M. Milot, *Laïcités sans frontières* (Paris: Éditions du Seuil, 2011). Author's translation.
8 M. Koenig, "Politics and Religion in European Nation-States: Institutional Varieties and Contemporary Transformations," in Bernhard Giesen and Daniel Suber, eds., *Religion and Politics: Cultural Perspectives* (Boston: Brill, 2005), 291–315.
9 T. Monood, "Moderate Secularism and Multiculturalism," *Politics*, Vol. 29, No. 1 (2009): 71–76.
10 E. Winter, "Us, Them, and Others: Reflections on Canadian Multiculturalism and National Identity at the Turn of the Twenty-First Century," *Canadian Review of Sociology*, Vol. 51, No. 2 (2014): 128–51.
11 D. Hervieu-Léger, "Multiple Religious Modernities: A New Approach to Contemporary Religiosity," in Eliezer Ben-Rafael and Yitzhak Sternberg, eds., *Comparing Modernities: Pluralism Versus Homogenity. Essays in Homage to Shmuel N. Eisenstadt* (Leiden: Brill, 2005), 336–37.
12 S. Lacombe, "French Canada: Rise and Decline of a Church-Nation," *Quebec Studies Journal*, No. 48 (autumn 2009 / winter 2010): 135–58; J.-P. Warren, "L'invention du Canada français : le rôle de l'Église catholique," *Balises et références. Acadies, francophonies*, in Martin Pâquet and Stéphane Savard, eds., (Ste-Foy, QC: Presses de l'Université Laval, 2007), 21–56; P.-A. Turcotte, "The National Church as a Historical Form of Church-Type: Elements of a Configurative Theorization," *Social Compass*, Vol. 59, No. 4 (2012): 525–38; J.-F. Laniel, "L'Église-nation canadienne-française au siècle des nationalités : regard croisé sur l'ultramontanisme et le nationalisme," *Études d'histoire religieuse*, Vol. 81, Nos. 1 et 2 (2015), 15–37.

13 E.-M. Meunier and J.-P. Warren, *Sortir de la « Grande noirceur ». L'horizon « personnaliste »* de la *Révolution tranquille* (Sillery: Éditions du Septentrion, 2002); M. Gauvreau, *The Catholic Origins of Quebec's Quiet Revolution, 1931–1970* (Montréal and Kingston: McGill-Queen's University Press), 2005.

14 E.-M. Meunier, *Le pari personnaliste : modernité et catholicisme au XXe siècle* (Saint-Laurent, QC: Fides, 2007).

15 P. Beyer, "The Mission of Quebec Ultramontanism: A Luhmannian Perspective," *Sociological Analysis*, Vol. 46, No. 1 (Spring 1985): 37–48.

16 D. Seljak, "Why the Quiet Revolution was 'Quiet': The Catholic Church's Reaction to the Secularization of Nationalism in Quebec after 1960," *CCHA Historical Studies*, Vol. 62 (1996): 109–24; E.-M. Meunier and J.-F. Laniel, « Congrès eucharistique international 2008. Nation et catholicisme culturel au Québec : signification d'une recomposition religio-politique », *Sciences religieuses/Studies in Religion*, Vol. 41, No. 4 (2012): 595–617.

17 G. Dussault, « Dimensions messianiques du catholicisme québécois au dix-neuvième siècle », W. Westfall, L. Rousseau, F. Harvey, and J. Simpson, eds., *Religion/Culture Comparative Canadian Studies*, Association des études canadiennes, Vol. VII (1985): 64–71.

18 D. Martin, "Sociology, Religion and Secularization: An Orientation," *Religion*, Vol. 25 (1995): 298; *A General Theory of Secularization* (New York: Harper & Row, 1979 [1978]).

19 F. Champion, « Entre laïcisation et sécularisation. Des rapports Église-État dans l'Europe communautaire », *Le Débat*, No. 77 (1993): 40–63.

20 P. Berger, G. Davie and Effie Fokas, *Religious America, Secular Europe? A Theme and Variations* (Aldershot and Burlington, Ashgate, 2008).

21 Ph. Portier, « Conclusion. Les laïcités à l'épreuve de la 'deuxième modernité' », Jean Baubérot, Micheline Milot, and Philippe Portier, eds.; *Laïcité, laïcités. Reconfigurations et nouveaux défis (Afrique, Amériques, Europe, Japon, Pays arabes)* (Paris: Éditions de la Maison des sciences de l'homme, 2014), 375–97.

22 S. Grammond, « Conceptions canadienne et québécoise des droits fondamentaux et de la religion : convergence ou conflit ? », *Revue juridique Thémis*, No. 43 (2009): 83.

23 Grammond, « Conceptions canadienne et québécoise des droits fondamentaux et de la religion », 105.

24 Grammond, « Conceptions canadienne et québécoise des droits fondamentaux et de la religion », 83.

25 E.-M. Meunier, J.-F. Laniel, and J.-C. Demers, « Permanence et recomposition de la 'religion culturelle' : aperçu socio-historique du catholicisme québécois (1970-2006) », in Robert Mager and Serge Cantin, eds., *Religion et modernité au Québec* (Québec: Presses de l'Université Laval, 2010), 79–128.

26 F.-A. Isambert, "La sécularisation interne du christianisme", *Revue française de sociologie*, Vol. 17, No. 4 (1976): 573–89.
27 C. Taylor, "Après *L'Âge séculier*," in Sylvie Taussig, ed., *Charles Taylor : Religion et sécularisation* (Paris: CNRS Éditions, 2014), 12.
28 J.-F. Laniel, "La *laïcité québécoise* est-elle achevée? Essai sur une petite nation, entre société neuve et république," in E.-Martin Meunier, ed., *Le Québec et ses mutations culturelles : sept questions pour l'avenir d'une société* (Ottawa: University of Ottawa Press, 2015), forthcoming.
29 N.J. Demerath, "The Rise of 'Cultural Religion' in European Christianity: Learning from Poland, Northern Ireland, and Sweden," *Social Compass*, Vol. 47, No. 1 (2000): 127–39; J.-F. Laniel, « Qu'en est-il de la 'religion culturelle'? Sécularisation, nation et imprégnation culturelle du christianisme," in S. Lefebvre, C. Béraud, and E.-M. Meunier, eds., *Catholicisme et cultures : Regards croisés Québec/France* (Québec and Rennes: Presses de l'Université Laval and Presses de l'Université de Rennes, 2015), 143–68.
30 E.-M. Meunier, J.-F. Laniel, and J.-C. Demers, « Permanence et recomposition de la 'religion culturelle' : aperçu socio-historique du catholicisme québécois (1970-2006) »; R. Lemieux, « Le catholicisme québécois : une question de culture », *Sociologie et sociétés*, Vol. 22, No. 2 (1990): 145–64.
31 Such a "civic" role for Catholicism could be said to be the work of abovementioned "personalists." A. Charron, « Catholicisme culturel et identité chrétienne », in Brigitte Caulier, ed., *Religion, sécularisation, modernité. Les expériences francophones en Amérique du Nord* (Québec: Presses de l'Université Laval, 1996), 157–90; M. Roy, *Une réforme dans la fidélité. La revue* Maintenant *(1962-1974) et la « mise à jour » du catholicisme québécois* (Québec: Presses de l'Université Laval, 2012).
32 Such a cultural relationship to religion is common in other liberal democracies, but is particularly vibrant in contemporary or historically stateless nations.
33 On that subject, the 2014 campaign was not about *laïcité* but about the spectre of a new referendum on Quebec's independence.
34 G. Bouchard, *L'interculturalisme : un point de vue Québécois* (Montréal: Boréal, 2012).

Chapter 3

1 Significant portions of this chapter have been extracted from the expert reports of Dr. J. Kent Donlevy and Dr. John F. Brosseau, attached to their affidavits in the matter of *Aspen View et al* v. *Alberta et al.*, Q.B. Action No. 0403 21814, with their consent.
2 Officially titled *An Act for the Relief of His Majesty's Roman Catholic Subjects*, 10 Geo 4, c 7.

3   25 Vict. c. 18.
4   30 & 31 Vict., c. 3.
5   Officially entitled *Order of Her Majesty in Council admitting Rupert's Land and the North Western Territory into the union*, dated the 23rd day of June, 1870.
6   33 Vict., c. 3.
7   4-5 Edw VII, c. 3 (Can).
8   4-5 Edw VII, c. 42 (Can).
9   Bonaventure Fagan, "Newfoundland and Labrador," in *Catholic Schools Across Canada: Into a New Millennium*, John J. Flynn, ed. (Toronto: Canadian Catholic School Trustees' Association, 2003).
10 Fagan, "Newfoundland and Labrador," under term 17 of the *Terms of Union*.
11 Officially titled *An Act for the Relief of His Majesty's Roman Catholic Subjects*, 10 Geo 4, c. 7.
12 Bishop Colin Campbell, "Maritime Provinces," in Flynn, *Catholic Schools Across Canada*, 43.
13 *Ex Parte Renaud* (1873), 14 NBR 273.
14 *Ex Parte Renaud*.
15 Douglas A. Schmeiser, *Civil Liberties in Canada* (London: Oxford University Press, 1964).
16 Campbell, "Maritime Provinces," 45.
17 *Maher v. Town of Portland*, PC 1874.
18 *Ex Parte Renaud*.
19 *Maher v. Town of Portland*.
20 (1873) 14 NBR 273.
21 Audrey S. Brent, "The Right to Religious Education and the Constitutional Status of Denominational Schools," *Saskatchewan Law Review*, 40 (1974): 239–67.
22 Brent, "The Right to Religious Education and the Constitutional Status of Denominational Schools."
23 Campbell, "Maritime Provinces," 48.
24 John J. Flynn, "Quebec," in Flynn, *Catholic Schools Across Canada*, 37.
25 C.B. Sissons, *Church & State in Canadian Education: An Historical Study* (Toronto: Ryerson Press, 1959), 13.
26 Sissons, *Church & State in Canadian Education*, 14–15.
27 Sissons, *Church & State in Canadian Education*, 18.
28 Sissons, *Church & State in Canadian Education*, 25.
29 Sissons, *Church & State in Canadian Education*, 25.

30 22 Vict. c. 64.
31 18 Vict. c. 131.
32 26 Vict. c. 5.
33 Franklin A. Walker, *Catholic Education and Politics in Upper Canada, Vol. 1: A Study of the Documentation Relative to the Origin of the Catholic Elementary Schools in the Ontario School System* (Toronto: The Federation of Catholic Education Associations of Ontario, 1955), 163, s. VIII & XIII.
34 Walker, *Catholic Education and Politics in Upper Canada*, Vol. 1, 250–87 (ss. 2, 3, 5, 6, 7 & 12).
35 *Tiny Roman Catholic Separate School Board v. R.*, [1928] 3 DLR 753, [1928] AC 363, 20.
36 9 Vict. c. 27, S.C. 1846, c. 27.
37 9 Vict. c. 27, 135.
38 *Hirsch v. Board of School Commissioners of Montreal*, [1928] 1 DLR 1041, [1928] AC 200.
39 *Quebec Association of Protestant School Boards v. Attorney-General of Quebec*, 21 DLR (4th) 36, 32 ACWS (2d) 173.
40 *Quebec Association of Protestant School Boards v. Attorney-General of Quebec.*
41 Walker, *Catholic Education and Politics in Upper Canada*, 147.
42 [1895] AC 202, 5 Cart BNA 156; see also Arthur S. Morton, *The History of the Canadian West to 1870–71* (Toronto: University of Toronto Press, 1973).
43 Correspondence from Mary Margaret MacKinnon, Guild Yule, August 13, 2015.
44 Correspondence from Mary Margaret MacKinnon.
45 Michael McAteer, "British Columbia," in Flynn, *Catholic Schools Across Canada*, 2.
46 Correspondence from Mary Margaret MacKinnon.
47 *Reference Re Bill 30, An Act to Amend the Education Act (Ont.)*, [1987] 1 SCR 1148.
48 *Constitution Act, 1867*, 30 & 31 Vict., c. 3, ss. 91–92, 93 (UK).
49 *Debates of the House of Commons of the Dominion of Canada*, 7th Parliament, 6th Session (January 2, 1896: March 13, 1896) (Ottawa: S.E. Dawson, 1896), 2719–97.
50 *Debates of the House of Commons of the Dominion of Canada*, 7th Parliament, 6th Session.
51 *Canadian Charter of Rights and Freedoms*, s. 2, Part I of *The Constitution Act, 1982*, being Schedule B to the *Canada Act 1982* (UK), 1982, c. 11, s. 29.
52 Ottawa: Government of Canada, 1982.
53 Donald C. Brock, "Manitoba," in Flynn, *Catholic Schools Across Canada*, 21.

54 Morton, *A History of the Canadian West*, 877; George F. Stanley, *The Birth of Canada: A History of the Riel Rebellions* (London: Longmans & Green, 1936), 70–147; *R v. Mercure*, 1 SCR 234, 48 DLR (4th) 1, where La Forest J., writing for the majority, stated: "impending changes were not viewed with favour by the people in the Territories, most of whom lived in the Red River area."

55 Morton, *A History of the Canadian West*, 903.

56 Morton, *A History of the Canadian West*, 903; Stanley, *The Birth of Canada*, 96.

57 Donald Creighton, *John A. Macdonald: The Young Politician, The Old Chieftain* (Toronto: University of Toronto Press, 1998), Vol. 2, 65–66; see also Sissons, *Church & State in Canadian Education*, 172.

58 Creighton, *John A. Macdonald*, Vol. 2, 5.

59 *Rupert's Land and North-Western Territory Order, 1870.*

60 *An Act for Enabling Her Majesty to accept a Surrender upon Terms of the Lands, Privileges, and Rights of "The Governor, and Company of Adventurers of England trading into Hudson's Bay" and for admitting the same into the Dominion of Canada*, 1868, 31 & 32 Vict. c. 105.

61 *An Act for Enabling Her Majesty to accept a Surrender*, 1869, 32 & 33 Vict. c. 3.

62 [1892] AC 445, 5 Cart BNA 32.

63 [1895] AC 202, 5 Cart BNA s. 22(2) 156.

64 [1895] AC 202, 5 Cart BNA s. 22(2) 156; Brock, "Manitoba," in Flynn, *Catholic Schools Across Canada*, 23.

65 SC 1869, 32–33 Vict. c. 3 (Can).

66 SC 1869, 32–33 Vict. c. 3 (Can); June 23, 1870.

67 38 Vict. c. 49.

68 RSC 1886 c. 50 s. 14.

69 David J. Bercuson, *One School System: Accommodating Religious Difference in Alberta's Public Schools. Alberta Public School Boards' Association v. Alberta (Attorney General)*, [1995] A.J. No. 171 (Q.B.), (1995) 198 A.R. 204 (Q.B.) 163 [1996] A.J. No. 704 (Q.B.); (1996) 42 Alta L.R. (3d) 443 (C.A.); (1998) 158 D.L.R. (4th) 267 (Alta Q.B.); (1998) D.L.R. (4th) 275 (Alta C.A.); [1999] S.C.C.A. No. 286, [2000] 1 S.C.R. 44; [2000] 2 S.C.R. 409; (see also Sandra M. Anderson, "Venerable Rights: Constitutionalizing Alberta's Schools, 1869–1905," in *Forging Alberta's Constitutional Framework*, Richard Connors and John M. Law, eds. (Edmonton: University of Alberta Press, 2005).

70 Anderson, *Venerable Rights*

71 31 WLR 82; 1915 CarswellSask 31.

72 David J. Hall, *Clifford Sifton, Vol. II: A Lonely Eminence* (Vancouver: University of British Columbia Press, 1985).
73 Evelyn Eager, "Separate Schools and the Cabinet Crisis of 1905," *Lakehead University Review* (Fall 1969).
74 David J. Bercuson, *One School System*, 26–27.
75 RSY 2002 c. 61.
76 See Richard Stuart, "Duff Pattaloo and the Yukon Schools Question of 1837," *Canadian Historical Review* 64 (1983): 25–44; T.A. Cory, *Re Proposed Transfer of Yukon Territory to the Province of British Columbia* (Justice Canada: PAC RG 85, vol. 880, file 8975A); *1939 Royal Commission on Dominion Provincial Relations* (Rowell-Sirois Commission, PAC, RG 85, vol. 880, file 8975).
77 SC 1875, c. 49.
78 SC 1880, 47 Vict. c. 23.
79 *Yellowknife Public Denominational District Education Authority v. Northwest Territories (Local Authorities Election Act, Returning Officer)* 2008 NWTCA 13, 304 DLR (4th), 149.
80 *Yellowknife Public Denominational District Education Authority v. Northwest Territories*
81 *Yellowknife Public Denominational District Education Authority v. Northwest* Territories; Flynn, "Quebec," in Flynn, *Catholic Schools Across Canada*, 41.
82 *Quebec (Attorney General) v. Greater Hull School Board*, [1984] 2 SCR 575, 15 DLR (4th) 651.
83 *Greater Montreal Protestant School Board v. Quebec*, [1989] 1 SCR 377, 57 DLR (4th) 521; *Reference re Education Act* (Quebec), [1993] 2 SCR 511, 105 DLR (4th) 266.
84 *Greater Montreal Protestant School Board v. Quebec*, [1989]; Flynn, "Quebec," in Flynn, 42.
85 Fagan, "Newfoundland and Labrador," in Flynn, *Catholic Schools Across Canada*..
86 *Hogan v. Newfoundland*, 166 Nfld & PEIR 161, 21 CPC (4th) 182.
87 *Hogan v. Newfoundland*, 166 Nfld & PEIR 161, 21 CPC (4th) 182.
88 Michael McAteer, "British Columbia," in Flynn, *Catholic Schools Across Canada*.
89 Especially important was the decision of *Calgary Board of Education v. A.G. Alberta*, [1980] 1 W.W.R. 347, [1981] 4 W.W.R. 187.
90 2000 SCC 45, [2000] 2 SCR 409.
91 See *Reference Re Bill 30, An Act to Amend the Education Act* [1987] 1 SCR 1148, 40 DLR (4th) 18.

92 Carl Matthews, S.J., and Anthony J. Barone, "Ontario," in Flynn, *Catholic Schools Across Canada*.
93 [2001] 1 S.C.R. 470, 2001 SCC 15.

Chapter 5

1 An excellent summary of the Catholic Church's position is found in the Congregation for the Doctrine of the Faith's Doctrinal Note *On Some Questions Regarding the Participation of Catholics in Political Life*, 2002: http://www.vatican.va/roman_curia/congregations/cfaith/documents/rc_con_cfaith_doc_20021124_politica_en.html (accessed August 14, 2015).
2 Second Vatican Council, Pastoral Constitution *Gaudium et spes*, 30.
3 John Paul II, Encyclical Letter *Veritatis splendor*, 84–85. Italics in original.
4 *Catechism of the Catholic Church*, no. 2358.
5 All of these issues have been topics of statements and pastoral letters of the Canadian Conference of Catholic Bishops over the past several decades.
6 Antonio Spadaro, "A Big Heart open to God: The Exclusive Interview with Pope Francis," *America*, September 30, 2013.
7 Debra Black, "Court strikes down Conservatives' cuts to refugee health-care coverage," *Toronto Star*, July 4, 2014.
8 Doctrinal Note *On Some Questions Regarding the Participation of Catholics in Political Life*, 7.
9 *Gaudium et spes*, 43.
10 *Gaudium et spes*, 43.

Chapter 6

1 The full text of this letter may be found at the Canadian Conference of Catholic Bishops website: http://www.cccb.ca/site/eng/media-room/official-texts/pastoral-letters/769-the-struggle-against-poverty-a-sign-of-hope-in-our-world (accessed June 19, 2015).
2 See Joe Gunn, "Muted and Maligned Voices: Public Justice and the Canadian Churches," *The Ecumenist* 47:4 (Winter 2010): 1–6. This anecdote is based on his recollection of events, which I also cite in *Ethical Being: A Catholic Guide to Contemporary Issues* (Ottawa: Novalis, 2013), 165–66.
3 Max Ehrenfreud, "Pope Francis's views on climate change put GOP candidates in a bind," *The Washington Post* (June 18, 2015): http://www.washingtonpost.com/blogs/wonkblog/wp/2015/06/18/wonkbook-pope-franciss-views-on-climate-change-put-catholic-gop-candidates-in-a-bind (accessed June 30, 2015).
4 See James Davison Hunter, *The Culture Wars: The Struggle to Define America* (New York: Basic Books, 1991). Writing at the end of the Reagan Revolution

in the United States, Hunter, a sociologist, argues that the profound domestic political disagreements of the early 1990s may be traced to different formulations and sources of moral authority. He referred to the factions as "orthodox" and "progressive."

5   One win for conservatives was *Burwell* v. *Hobby Lobby* (2014), which allowed closely held for-profit companies to claim an exemption on religious grounds from the *Affordable Care Act* (ACA). The decision was based on an interpretation of the *Religious Freedom Restoration Act* (RFRA). For many culture warriors, the ACA is an infringement upon their personal liberty and should be ruled unconstitutional. However, *King* v. *Burwell* (2015) affirmed that subsidies established by states to help citizens access insurance through the various exchanges – in effect, the Court affirmed the constitutionality of the ACA. In *Obergefell* v. *Hodges* (2015), the Supreme Court ruled that all states must recognize same-sex marriage under the Fourteenth Amendment, the due process amendment, which was also the basis for the Court's decision in *Loving* v. *Virginia* (1967), which allowed inter-racial marriage.

6   David Brooks, "The Next Culture War," *The New York Times* (June 30, 2015), A23.

7   Marci McDonald, *The Armageddon Factor: The Rise of Christian Nationalism in Canada* (Toronto: Random House of Canada, 2010), 359.

8   Molly Worthen, "Onward Christian Nationalists," *The Globe and Mail* (May 14, 2010).

9   Hugh Heclo, *Christianity and American Democracy* (Cambridge: Harvard University Press, 2007), 29. This section is based on my review of Heclo's book, which appeared as "Christianity and the American Republic," *The Ecumenist* 45:4 (Fall 2008): 22–24.

10 Jose Casanova recognizes secularism in both its practical terms (e.g., separation of church and state) and ideological terms (e.g., religion is intolerant). As a sociologist, he also notes that secularism has become shorthand for a type of self-sufficiency that does not allow for any transcendence beyond the secular spheres. For a fuller discussion, see Jose Casanova, *Public Religions in the Modern World* (Chicago: University of Chicago Press, 1994). For a definition of "secularization," see Peter Berger, *The Sacred Canopy* (New York: Anchor Books, 1967), 107. According to Berger, secularization is "the process by which sectors of society and culture are removed from the domination of religious institutions and symbols."

11 David Seljak, "Trudeau and the Privatization of Religion," in *The Hidden Pierre Elliott Trudeau: The Faith Behind the Politics*, John English, Richard Gwyn, and P. Whitney Lackenbauer, eds. (Ottawa: Novalis, 2004), 51.

12 Heclo, *Christianity and American Democracy*, 79.

13 William E. Connolly, *Why I Am Not a Secularist* (Minneapolis: University of Minnesota Press, 1999), 24.

14 U.S. Catholic Bishops, *The Christian in Action*, No. 11, 1948; reprinted in Hugh J. Nolan, ed., *Pastoral Letters of the American Hierarchy, 1792–1970* (Huntington, IN: Our Sunday Visitor, 1971).

15 John F. Kennedy, "Address of Senator John F. Kennedy to the Greater Houston Ministerial Association," September 12, 1960. Transcripts and video are available online at the John F. Kennedy Presidential Library, www.jfklibrary.org (accessed May 14, 2015). This section is a slightly revised version of a text that appears in Kline, *The Ethical Being*.

16 Habermas has made this argument in numerous places. See, for example, Jürgen Habermas, "'The Political': The Rational Meaning of a Questionable Inheritance of Political Theology," in Judith Butler, Jürgen Habermas, Charles Taylor, and Cornel West, *The Power of Religion in the Public Sphere*, Eduardo Mendieta and Jonathan Vanantwerpen, eds. (New York: Columbia University Press, 2011), 27.

17 Here is not the place to elucidate the many challenges to this answer. However, I would note that truth and reconciliation commissions involving religious actors, religiously based land claim legal challenges, and claims of political sovereignty on religious grounds have not fared well in many secular processes. Indeed, I have written on this elsewhere: Megan Shore and Scott Kline, "The Ambiguous Role of Religion in the South African Truth and Reconciliation Commission," *Peace and Change* 31 (2006): 309–22. Also see Megan Shore, *Religion and Conflict Resolution: Christianity and South Africa's Truth and Reconciliation Commission* (Burlington, VT: Ashgate Publishing, 2009).

Chapter 7

1 "Senators call for new blood on committee dealing with audit fallout," *CBC News*, May 15, 2015: https://ca.news.yahoo.com/senators-call-blood-committee-dealing-090000257.html (accessed May 15, 2015).

2 "Top Celebrity Scandals of 2014," *The Toronto Star*, January 4, 2015.

3 Starbucks dives into U.S. race relations with "#RaceTogether campaign," *The Globe and Mail*, May 18, 2015: http://www.theglobeandmail.com/news/world/starbucks-dives-into-us-race-relations-issue-with-racetogether-campaign/article23525794 (accessed May 18, 2015).

4 Thomas Williams, "Saint Anselm," *The Stanford Encyclopedia of Philosophy* (Spring 2013), Edward N. Zalta, ed. http://plato.stanford.edu/archives/spr2013/entries/anselm (accessed May 16, 2015).

5 Charles Taylor, *A Secular Age* (Cambridge, MA: Belknap Press of Harvard University Press, 2007), 191.

6 Taylor, *A Secular Age,* 185.
7 Taylor, *A Secular Age,* 187.
8 Susan Delacourt, *Shopping for Votes: How Politicians Choose Us and We Choose Them* (Madeira Park, BC: Douglas and McIntyre, 2013), 327.
9 See Bronwen Wilson and Paul Yachnin, *Making Publics in Early Modern Europe: People, Things, Forms of Knowledge* (New York: Routledge–Taylor and Francis, 2010).

 This volume speaks to the early development of the "public." What may be useful for our current conversation is to reclaim the dynamism of what it takes to create and sustain a public. Many faith leaders today need to better understand this concept.

10 I believe this concept traces its origins to Dr. R. Ninian Smart, a pioneer in secular religious studies.
11 In my lectures, I have made this comment many times to distinguish the nature of what I have termed "life questions" from the wide range of important, but less ultimate, questions people often face. Space does not permit a lengthy treatment of these. In short, they are questions about that which we value ultimately. Matters of peace and justice form an important constellation of life questions in some contexts. In other contexts (often more affluent situations), our life questions may focus on meaning (e.g., Why am I here? Who am I? What is my purpose in life?). Some of the best responses to "life questions" are those found in the Wisdom books of the Bible.
12 Ron Duty, "Moral deliberation in a Public Lutheran Church," *Dialog: A Journal of Theology* (Winter 2006), 338–55.
13 See Lewis Smedes, *Choices: Making Right Decisions in a Complex World* (New York: Harper and Row, 1986).
14 Gibson Winter, "Introduction," in *Social Ethics: Issues in Ethics and Society,* Gibson Winter, ed. (New York: Harper and Row, 1968), 6.
15 Williams, "Saint Anselm."
16 Reinhold Niebuhr, *An Interpretation of Christian Ethics* (New York: Living Age Books, 1960), 15.
17 Reginald Bibby, *Beyond the Gods and Back: Religion's Demise and Rise and Why It Matters* (Lethbridge, AB: Project Canada Books, 2011), 38.

 Bibby also points out that "In a recent poll of 84 countries, the Gallup organization confirmed the fact that meaning does not require religion ... The gods are not indispensable to finding purpose. But they do not have many equals when it comes to addressing with certainty what happens when we die." (134-35).

18 Bibby, *Beyond the Gods and Back,* 122.

19 "Organized religion on the decline? Growing number of Canadians 'spiritual but not religious'?" *The National Post*, December 21, 2012.
20 "Organized religion on the decline?" *National Post*, December 21, 2012.
21 Peter C. Newman, *The Canadian Revolution* (Toronto: Viking Press, 1995), 103.
22 "Canadians attend weekly religious services less than 20 years ago," Statistics Canada http://www.statcan.gc.ca/pub/89-630-x/2008001/article/10650-eng.htm (accessed May 20, 2015).
23 Robert D. Putnam, *Bowling Alone: The Collapse and Revival of American Community* (New York: Simon and Shuster, 2000).
24 *Canadians on Citizenship: The First National Survey on What it Means to be a Citizen in Canada, Summary Report*. http://maytree.com/wp-content/uploads/2012/02/Canadians-on-Citizenship-Summary-Report.pdf (accessed May 19, 2015).
25 Bibby, *Beyond the Gods and Back,* 61.
26 David Pfrimmer, "Stewards of the Public Commons: A Vocation for Government and Church," in *Communion, Responsibility, Accountability: Responding as a Lutheran Communion to Neoliberal Globalization*, Karen Bloomquist, ed. (Geneva: Lutheran World Federation, Documentation 50, 2004), 235–50.
27 Martin Marty, *The Public Church* (New York: Crossroad, 1981), 3ff.
28 Jürgen Moltmann, *God for a Secular Society* (London: SCM Press, 1999), 1.
29 Adrienne Clarkson, *Belonging: The Paradox of Citizenship* (Toronto: House of Anansi Press, 2014), 41.
30 The following articles illustrate some of the loss of confidence by Canadians.

Janyce McGregor, "Canadians lack confidence governments can solve issues," *CBC News* (July 25, 2012). http://www.cbc.ca/news/politics/canadians-lack-confidence-governments-can-solve-issues-1.1200130 (accessed May 18, 2015).

Matthew Coutts, "Canadians don't have faith in their leaders, new Yahoo-Leger poll shows," *Yahoo Canada News* (November 13, 2013). https://ca.news.yahoo.com/canadians-don-t-have-faith-in-their-leaders--yahoo-leger-poll-shows-185636826.html (accessed May 20, 2015).

Theresa Tedesco, "Canadians' trust in corporate leaders drops to lowest level since 2008, report says," *The Financial Post* (February. 3, 2015). http://webcache.googleusercontent.com/search?q=cache:35mQRm2ROSwJ:business.financialpost.com/news/fp-street/canadians-trust-in-corporate-leaders-drops-to-lowest-level-since-2008-report-says+&cd=1&hl=en&ct=clnk&gl=us&client=safari (accessed August 19, 2015).

31 Michael Swan, "Canadians are becoming ambivalent on religion," *The Catholic Register* (April 2, 2015). http://www.catholicregister.org/item/19967-canadians-are-becoming-ambivalent-on-religion (accessed August 19, 2015).
32 David Pfrimmer, "Developing a Public Hermeneutic for the Future of Theological Education," *Dialog: A Journal of Theology* (December 2011): 368–72.
33 Ronald A. Heifetz, *Leadership Without Easy Answers* (Cambridge, MA: Harvard University Press, 1994).
34 See Delacourt, *Shopping for Votes*.
35 Alison Loat and Michael MacMillan, *Tragedy in the Commons* (Toronto: Random House, 2014), 213.
36 Chris Hedges, *Death of the Liberal Class* (New York: Nation Books, 2010), 8–9.
37 Elizabeth May, *Losing Confidence: Power, Politics and the Crisis of Canadian Democracy* (Toronto: McClelland and Stewart, 2006), 9.
38 Dr. Christopher Ross is a professor of religion and culture at Wilfrid Laurier University in Waterloo, ON. He shared this view with me in a gathering at Waterloo Lutheran Seminary.
39 Michael Ignatieff, *Blood and Belonging: Journeys into the New Nationalism* (Toronto: Viking Press, 1993).
40 Manfred Max-Neef, *Outside Looking In: Experiences in Barefoot Economics* (London: Zed Books, 1992).
41 Carol Goar, "Loss of faith imperils charities," *The Toronto Star* (May 5, 2006), cited in Reginald Bibby, *Beyond the Gods and Back*, 161.
42 Bibby, *Beyond the Gods and Back*, 160.
43 Douglas John Hall, *The Canada Crisis: A Christian Perspective* (Toronto: Anglican Book Centre, 1980), 114.